Preparing to Teach God's Word

A handbook for leaders, teachers, and others aspiring to reach people for God

Claudia J. Finlay-Parker Ph.D.

Copyright © 2005 by Claudia J. Finlay-Parker Ph.D.

Preparing to Teach God's Word
by Claudia J. Finlay-Parker Ph.D.

Printed in the United States of America

ISBN 1-59781-023-1

All rights reserved solely by the author. The author guarantees all contents are original and do not infringe upon the legal rights of any other person or work. No part of this book may be reproduced in any form without the permission of the author. The views expressed in this book are not necessarily those of the publisher.

The author took care to protect and disclose copyrighted material. I will welcome comments that may identify and describe opinions not correctly credited.

All scripture quotations were taken from the Holy Bible, New American Standard Version. Copyright © 1977 by The Lockman Foundation, laHabra, California.

www.xulonpress.com

Acknowledgements

I thank God for health, strength, enthusiasm, courage, and all the other resources I needed to complete this handbook. The handbook project first emerged while I served on the Life Builders committee at Beulah Alliance Church with Melody Coutts (now Kilbank), its chair. Members of that committee provided encouragement, read early drafts, and offered valuable comments. My husband Phillip, a lawyer, also donated some of his time to read early drafts and made constructive recommendations. I am very grateful for Pastor Dave Tjart's support. He was kind enough to read later drafts and even passed one of them to his friend, another educator, for suggestions. Pastor Dale Durie remarked on all the work that went into the preparation of the manuscript.

To all those people who came into my life, prayer and care groups, Bible- study group leaders, and Sunday school teachers, I appreciated your guidance along the way. I credit all of you for your part in encouraging me as I continue to mature as a Christian.

I owe much gratitude to my senior pastor, Pastor Keith Taylor, whose sermons influenced my writing and contributed to my stance in this handbook. Adult educators whose research supplied substance for the text, also deserves merit. I feel compelled to recognize the staff at Xulon Press for leading me through the publication process. Special acknowledgement is due to the Lockman Foundation for its New American Standard Version of the Holy Bible which I used extensively in writing this handbook.

I could not have completed this handbook without family

support; from my husband and sons, and in particular, my sister Yvonne, who always was excited about the project and constantly prayed with me. I am so grateful that my parents brought me up in a Christian home, where I experienced the love of God and where they taught me to depend on Him for everything. This is why I dedicated this handbook to my mother, the late Mrs. Aleitha Finlay.

My father's favourite Bible verse is "Commit your way to the Lord." I believe He directed me to write this handbook with the guidance of His Holy Spirit.

Dedication

To my mother, who was my first teacher, and to all those people aspiring to bring others to a fuller understanding of the love of God and the reality that God's way is the only way to wisdom.

All scripture is inspired by God and profitable for teaching, for reproof, for correction, for training in righteousness; so that the man of God may be adequate, equipped for every good work. (2 Timothy 3:16-17)

Table of Contents

PREFACE .... **xi**

ABOUT THE AUTHOR .... **xv**

CHAPTER 1
   INTRODUCTION TO THE HOLISTIC APPROACH......**17**
      Introduction 19
      Definitions 20
      Rationale 21
         Scriptural Reference 21
      The Calling 22
         Preparation 24
      A Holistic Approach 25
      Organization of the Manual 26
         Spiritual 26
         Emotional, Intuitive, and Relational 27
         Physical 27
         Intellectual 27
      Organization of the Chapters 28
      Chapter Summary 28

CHAPTER 2
SPIRITUAL PREPARATION 31
Evidence of God's Presence..................................33
Signs and Wonders..34
Reliance of God 35
- Scripture Reference....................................36
- Scripture Preparation Steps.......................38
- Spiritual Exercise.......................................39

Chapter Summary 40

CHAPTER 3
EMOTIONAL PREPARATION..41
The Greatest Commandment 44
- Preparing Emotionally...............................45

Building Trust 46
Know Your Audience...47
Dealing With Feelings 48
- Scripture References..................................49
- Emotional Preparation Steps......................51
- Emotional Exercise 52

Chapter Summary 54

CHAPTER 4
PHYSICAL PREPARATION 55
Running the Race...58
Environmental Preparation 58
Physical Concerns..60
- Scripture Reference....................................61
- Physical Preparation Steps........................62
- Physical Exercise 63

Chapter Summary 65

CHAPTER 5
INTELLECTUAL PREPARATION 67
Learning and Teaching...70
- Teaching...70
- Learning 71

Adult Education 72
Andragogy vs. Pedagogy 73
Adult Learners Have Certain Characteristics...............74
Learning Styles 75
Perceptual versus Structural Learners.........................76
Dependent, Independent and Collaborative 77
Kolb's Experiential Model 78
Transformative Learning..79
Learning Activities..81
Learning Objectives 82
Delivery Methods 82
Presentation 84
Using Technology 85
Student Evaluation 86
Teacher Evaluation 87
Content..87
    Scripture References 89
    Intellectual Preparation Steps 90
    Intellectual Exercise 91
Chapter Summary 94

CHAPTER 6
SUMMARY AND CONCLUSION 95
God's Gifts and Promises..97
Purpose Revisited 98
Lesson in a Nutshell..98
Depending on Him 100
Scripture References 100
The End of the Journey 102
Chapter Summary 103
Closing Exercise 104
Conclusion 105

REFERENCES 107

APPENDIX 1
A NEW BEGINNING..
INTRODUCTION ....
A New Beginning...
Presentation..
Discussion Questions ....
Application...
Exercise...
Follow up ....
Growth and Application...

Preface

Orientation to any organization, including churches or schools, means adapting a position with reference to circumstances or ideals stipulated for that entity. This is no different at Christian churches that have a vision, mission, philosophy, goals, and objectives. For instance, one must understand ideals so that he or she would respect and promote them. At most churches, there is a mission, a vision, and a Statement of Faith, all of which drive the direction of members and adherents of the church. Overall, church administration wants to encourage the Christian way of life and the propagation of the gospel of Jesus Christ and God's will for Christians everywhere. At my church, we want to become "a loving community of committed followers of Christ."

This means that as Christians, God must be at the centre of our lives, and we should show this by emulating His love for us. We want to share His love in our homes as well as in our communities. The mission at my church, Beulah Alliance is:

'To reach, teach, and equip people to know, love, and serve Jesus Christ."

Reaching includes making an effort or going the extra mile to seek and care for others. To do this we must dedicate some time and effort to teaching. Teaching entails delivering the good news in such a manner that people would understand it and be willing to accept it. Equipping refers to the tools that teachers and leaders may use to facilitate learning, knowing, and serving God.

Keeping a vision and mission in mind will allow teachers and leaders at churches and other Christian organizations to stay focused on the goals of God's church and God's will, as they present God's word to those who are willing to hear it.

Churches' statements of faith explain their beliefs and boundaries. These statements define the limitless love of God and His gift to His people. For instance, Beulah Alliance Church distinguishes its values and differentiates them from the values that other Christian denominations may emphasize. Its administration clarifies to members and adherents the type of relationship to be attained with our Lord, and teaches how to simplify the connection between God and His people as they choose to illuminate the true Light of the World. The goal of this handbook is to help and encourage those who want to spread the "good news" of salvation. Being an experienced adult educator gave me the impetus to attempt this project, which has now become part of my life's journey.

My journey actually began much earlier when my parents brought me up in the fear and admonishment of our Lord. I taught my children as the Lord our God has instructed. Now it was time for me to embark on this project. I wanted to use my God-given skills and experience for the benefit of the congregation of God and those seeking Him.

In addition, having accepted salvation and the gift of grace, and through the leading of the Holy Spirit, I felt moved to share my passion for learning through teaching and trying to reach others for Christ. It is with this background that I endeavoured to write a handbook, one that I hope would facilitate teaching the good news of salvation and its application in everyday life.

This handbook addresses several levels of preparation for teaching, reaching and sharing God's word with people. It presents a holistic approach to teaching, specifying spiritual, emotional, physical, and intellectual dimensions of teaching preparation. It provides some instructional tips that will enhance teaching and learning. If you are seeking to understand some aspects of the Christian lifestyle or to teach adults, this handbook may be of interest to you. You can use it as a personal devotional or for professional development as a

Christian educator if you are interested in holistic teaching methods.

The information provided herein comes from searching the scriptures, reading and research, training, and experience in education. The writer, though not a Bible scholar, has read a limited number of scholarly religious writings.

About the Author

I was born in Grenada, West Indies, the first of eight children, four boys and four girls. Our parents brought us up in a Christian home. I accepted the Lord at an early age and followed His example of baptism at age eleven. According to the Plymouth Brethren way, I participated in the "Breaking of Bread" and young adult classes. After completing high school at St. George's in Grenada, I immigrated to Canada..

In Montreal, I became close friends with members of the Pentecostal faith and participated in services at Verdun Pentecostal Church. It was when I was attending university in Montreal that I met my husband, Phillip.

Phillip and I were married at the Westmont Baptist Church. We left soon afterwards for Barbados, where I was associated with the Brethren Assembly. Our first son was born in Barbados and dedicated to the Lord. We returned to Montreal, and shortly afterwards we made our home in Edmonton, Alberta, Canada. We found Beulah Alliance Church and Pastor Alton. Phil and I were first involved in Cradle Care and Children's Church. Our second son was born in Edmonton and dedicated to the Lord at Beulah Alliance Church. Our young sons attended Wee College and Children's Church. A third son arrived later and was dedicated at Beulah Alliance Church.

I started my work life in Canada as an accountant, first in

private practice and afterwards in public practice. After our first son was born, I decided motherhood was very important, and I followed my mother's example, which was to care for my young children at home. Being a Certified Management Accountant (CMA) with a Bachelor of Commerce Degree, I wanted to keep current so did some part-time accounting work at home. As my youngest grew older and began attending full time school, I began to teach at a postsecondary institution. I began my teaching career in the fall of 1983 on a part-time basis, and in January 1987, I accepted a full-time instructor's position. To improve myself, reduce nervousness, capture my audience, and remain calm, I pursued a Diploma in Adult Education, a master's degree in Education, and a Ph.D. in Educational Administration and Leadership.

My personal philosophy of teaching encouraged me to accommodate many learning styles and to satisfy as many learners as possible. My holistic approach allowed me to reach many participants.

I pursued this approach as I wrote this teaching handbook, hoping it would be useful to those who teach God's message of love, particularly those who lead Bible study classes.

CHAPTER 1

Introduction to the Holistic Approach

He gave some as apostles, and some as prophets, and some as evangelists, and some as pastors and teachers, for the equipping of the saints for the work of service, to the building up of the body of Christ. (Ephesians 4:11-12)

This chapter provides an overview of the handbook including:

>Introduction
>Definitions of teaching and related terms
>Rationale for the manual
>The calling
>A holistic approach
>Organization of the manual
>Organization of the chapters

INTRODUCTION

The Christian faith is very relevant in this dynamic age when more and more people are turning away from God and choosing secular humanism to resolve everyday problems. True Christians can vouch that Christian faith is not only essential but also applicable to all life situations. Teaching the Christian faith is particularly important in this post-modern period because the whole world seems to be turning upside down. The secular community seems to ignore values and morals or to give them very little attention. To counter this trend and be obedient, Christians must encourage propagation of God's teachings. Effectively implementing this teaching requires more men and women who are called to be fully equipped to teach God's word.

The purpose of this handbook is to introduce some teaching techniques and to provide some scriptural recommendations for those people who are preparing to teach adults, lead a Bible study, or otherwise reach people for God. The handbook focuses on planning to teach effectively. It is limited to an introduction to teaching adults and attempts to use simple rather than technical language where practicable. The handbook does not discuss any specific course content and is therefore general in nature, and more of a guide for teaching and learning. The Holy Bible, New American Standard Version, is the main source of reference. It also utilizes references to contemporary leaders in the field of adult education.

This handbook proposes only one of the methods of conceiving, planning and delivering Christian education. The project was necessary because literature in this area was scarce. Introducing this handbook on teacher preparation is therefore very timely.

For clarification, here are descriptions of some terms used in this handbook.

DEFINITIONS

"Andragogy" is the art of teaching adults.

"Affective domain" refers to knowledge that includes values, beliefs, emotions, and attitudes.

"Cognitive domain" means knowledge (for example, knowing definitions).

"Psycho-motor domain" deals with knowledge of physical skills.

"Taxonomy" refers to classification of knowledge levels.

"Teachers" is synonymous with "leaders" and "facilitators" and conveys the same meaning. Similarly, in this handbook, "students" is synonymous with "learners" and/or "participants."

"Active learning" is learning through experience. It is part of collaborative group work as students and teachers learn together.

"Transformative learning" is learning that produces change. "It shapes people. They are different afterwards in ways both they and others can recognize the change" (Clark 1995).

In "Collaborative learning", students gain some knowledge together with or without a teacher in the classroom. The facilitator or leader is not the only source or provider of information. Participants are not just receivers of information, but add or make knowledge (Bosworth and Hamilton, 1994)

The rest of the chapter presents a discussion of *the calling* of teachers, followed by a definition of teaching and learning. This discussion is followed by a layout of the organization of the manual. A dialogue on a holistic approach to teaching adults (recommended by Griffin 1993) shows how spiritual, emotional, relational, physical, intuitive, intellectual and logical capabilities affect adult learning.

RATIONALE

One may believe that teacher orientation should begin by focusing on teaching styles, methods, presentation, and evaluation, but there are other areas of preparation to consider. These areas of preparation involve having a teaching philosophy that is not static but develops as teachers mature and improve their methods. Teachers, take caution, since teaching is a phenomenon that can make an impressionable mark on students' minds or change someone's outlook on life. It is, therefore, essential for teachers to prepare holistically for the job. That means one should prepare spiritually and prayerfully as well as emotionally, physically, relationally, intuitively, and intellectually as they look to God for guidance. Teachers need to make a good impression on others' lives as they influence their students' thought processes. This handbook will focus on the many aspects of preparation for providing Christian education and responding to the great commission to reach others for Christ. For this reason, the Holy Bible is the main reference and source of information. Although other sources of information include experts on adult education principles and of current adult education thought, much emphasis is focused on scriptural references.

SCRIPTURE REFERENCE

Ephesians 4:11-12 provides for some spiritual callings specifying evangelists, pastors, and teachers, all engaged in spreading the gospel of Jesus Christ. Specifically, God has called people to propagate the gospel. Jesus wanted His disciples to spread the gospel. Confirmation of these callings is recorded in the books of Mathew, Mark, and Luke, as follows:

> And He said to them, "Go into all the world and preach the gospel to all creation." (Mark 16:15)

> Go and proclaim everywhere the kingdom of God.

(Luke 9:60)

Go therefore and make disciples of all the nations...
teaching them to observe all that I commanded you.
(Mathew 28:19-20)

These statements are direct orders or commands that Jesus gave to his disciples.

King David in the Old Testament wanted to spread the good news too. He said:

Proclaim good tidings of His salvation from day to day. Tell of His glory among the nations; His wonderful deeds among all the peoples: For great is the Lord, and greatly to be praised. (1 Chronicles 16: 23-25)

Those people who answer the call to teach are fulfilling this commandment in obedience to the great commission. God specifically called people for a special type of service, and they need to be equipped for it. Let us now turn our attention to this calling.

THE CALLING

Have you ever wondered why you seem to be at the right place at the right time to experience or witness some memorable occasion, to accept a position, or to be involved in an activity? What may have been the reason for you being there that day? You were perhaps destined to be there because God had placed you in that position or circumstance for a purpose. God may call you to do something, to make a difference in this world.

Webster's dictionary describes a *calling* as a vocation or profession. However, it may be an opportunity you have to make a difference or an impression on someone's life. Paul the apostle recognized that God called him to preach, and he reiterated this several times. In Romans 1:15 he said, "I am eager to preach the gospel to you also who are in Rome." Paul admitted to baptizing a few people. He acknowledged in 1 Corinthians 1:17, "For Christ did not send me to baptize, but to preach the gospel," and in Ephesians 3:8 he states, "To me, the very least of all the saints, this grace was given, to preach to the Gentiles the unfathomable riches of Christ." So although Paul could baptize, he was called to preach. He was a preacher and a teacher. Paul accepted his callings and was obedient to the Holy Spirit. The apostle Paul spoke of many other spiritual gifts. Paul explained:

> Since we have gifts that differ according to the grace given to us, each of us is to exercise them accordingly: if prophesy, according to the proportion of his faith; if service, in his serving; or he who teaches, in his teaching. (Romans 12:6-7)

And again,

> As each one has received a special gift, employ it in serving one another as good stewards of the manifold grace of God (1 Peter 4:10).

Although few people are preachers, most can contribute towards the propagation of the gospel. Those called to be teachers must take this calling very seriously. James warned:

> Let not many of you become teachers, my brethren, knowing that as such we will incur a stricter judgment. For we all stumble in many ways; if anyone does not stumble in what he says, he a perfect man. (James 3:1-2)

Human beings will never be perfect; as it states in Romans 3:23, "for all have sinned and fall short of the glory of God." Fortunately, "the Spirit Himself intercedes for us" and "the Spirit also helps our weakness" (Romans 8:26). Nevertheless, as human beings, teachers must strive to do their best with the gifts that the Lord has bestowed upon them, and they must also consider being properly equipped for teaching.

Preparation

Teachers need to determine and plan their teaching strategy. (Chapter 5 deals with teaching strategy). A good plan will not only enhance teaching but also learning. Planning includes setting goals and objectives. It takes into consideration teachers' values. Teachers must also choose some form or forms of teaching methods. Teachers must determine what works for them in a classroom setting. Evaluations are required so that teachers will know when they meet their goals. They must choose or develop a curriculum, select materials, and consider classroom activities.

Teachers must study their course content and be very comfortable with it. In addition, they must consider their audience in deciding on teaching methods for adults. The approach to teaching depends on the teacher's philosophy. Some teachers prefer the didactic method, others the relational method, or the lecture method. These methods are not mutually exclusive so a combination of methods may accomplish a teacher's goals. A teacher will have to choose the method that best suits the student participants, the subject, the environment, and his or her teaching philosophy.

Teachers must make decisions after considering their audiences and their needs, expectations and goals. Teachers must determine the differences in their audiences; how they want to participate in learning; their learning styles and preferences. When teachers consider preferences and combine them with teaching methods, delivery is effective. Decisions depend on considerations of types of audiences' preferences and their class participation, in corroboration with their expectations. As discussed earlier, the whole person must be involved in teaching and learning, so a holistic approach may be appropriate. A holistic approach may accomplish the goals of reaching and helping people mature in Christ.

A HOLISTIC APPROACH

Advocates of a holistic approach to learning emphasize that this approach will enhance teaching and learning at every level. This approach will engage the whole person including his or her past. As people reflect on experiences, they could make a connection to new experiences and new learning.

Some people think that they learn logically and sequentially, but studies have shown that is not the only way people learn. How a person learns will affect how that person teaches. Since there are several learning styles, there are several teaching styles. Since teaching involves helping others to learn, teachers need to consider all aspects of teaching and learning.

Griffin (1993, in Barer-Stein and Draper) suggests that using one teaching or learning method is like playing a one-string guitar. Of course, a guitar has six strings and each is important for good unified tone and high-quality music. Our bodies consist of several parts that have very important functions. The body of Christ is also made up of many parts, each of which performs specific functions. Each part is as important as each string of a guitar. Griffin used a guitar as a metaphor to describe all aspects of teaching. She named each string of this symbolic guitar as either logical, emotional, relational, physical, metaphoric or intuitive, or spiritual. Each of these proverbial "strings" represents an aspect of learning from a biblical perspective. Focusing on each string is like attending to the whole person. Griffin (1993) emphasized the use of all capabilities which would elevate learning to another level making it "fuller, more exciting and beautiful" (p. 117) because this would engage the whole person.

Griffin's holistic approach to teaching is not only a good fit for secular teaching but lends itself remarkably well to the application of biblical teaching. The strings of the proverbial guitar are combined in this handbook and discussed from a biblical perspective in four chapters. This handbook begins with the spiritual string, because Christians put God first in everything (Chapter 2). The emotional and intuitive strings refer to relational considerations (Chapter 3). Physical concerns come next (Chapter 4) and finally the handbook concludes with the rational or logical strings, including the theoretical and intellectual strings (Chapter 5) and ends with a concluding chapter (Chapter 6). People with the gift or calling to teach may find each "string" useful. Some people will particularly need to use each "string" at one time or another to attain the goal of reaching others for Christ. Each proverbial string addresses preparation needs of teachers and leaders. A discussion of each string and the organizational plan for this handbook follows.

ORGANIZATION OF THE MANUAL

This handbook provides some Bible references and steps that may encourage and improve learning and teaching, and will hopefully make Christian educators more successful in reaching others for Christ. A holistic approach as recommended by Griffin follows, with each chapter emphasizing spiritual, emotional, intuitive and relational, physical and intellectual considerations.

In each chapter, discussion precedes biblical support, followed by preparation steps and then an exercise section to reinforce planning in specific areas. A summary of each proverbial string follows. The first considered is the spiritual string.

Spiritual

Chapter two addresses the spiritual string. The world speaks of spirituality in a different context from God's people. They focus on spiritual beings. Christians accept the Holy Spirit as the Comforter who came to be with them until the Lord returns for his people. It is essential that teachers seek the fruit of the Spirit to nurture their spiritual health. God wants people to be continually striving towards spiritual health and growth as part of the body of Christ. The bible teaches that the Holy Spirit will lead people into all truths and accompany people along life's way. The filling with the Holy Spirit will affect how teachers respond emotionally to various stimuli. Responses will depend on emotions and a person's viewpoint at a particular time.

Emotional, Intuitive, and Relational

Understanding different personalities may help teachers and leaders discover how each personality type may prefer to learn. Chapter three emphasizes emotional preparation for teaching adults. States of mind, as well as external influences, have an emotional and intuitive effect on people who try to react rationally to situations. "And so those who have been chosen of God, holy and beloved, put on a heart of compassion, kindness, humility gentleness and patience (Colossians 3: v.12).

Teaching by itself is a stressful endeavour; one needs to be calm and emotionally ready to do a good job. Being enthusiastic enhances teaching and learning. Teachers need to be excited about what they teach and to be committed, by putting their whole heart and strength into it. In addition to emotional preparation, teachers need to ensure their physical state as well as the physical environment is prepared for teaching and learning.

Physical

Chapter four addresses physical preparation for teaching adults. Physical strength also contributes towards teaching effectiveness. Physical includes physical preparation of the environment where learning must take place. Adults learn best in a bright, comfortable, non-threatening environment. For example, adult educators recommend a round table seating arrangement. Therefore, preparation of the classroom and environment are also vital considerations when teaching adults to ensure that teachers and adult learners appear as equals. To treat adults as equals, a teacher should present himself or herself as a facilitator, and students as participants in the learning process. Proper preparation allows respect in the classroom or meeting place. The use of many teaching methods also facilitates learning. Intellectual preparation for delivering the course content facilitates learning, understanding, and teaching.

Intellectual

Intellectual preparation fosters effective teaching. Chapter five expands on this aspect of teacher training. Teachers need to be involved with the subject and interact with it. In other words, they have to be very familiar with the subject, being able to explain its usefulness, strengths, weaknesses and application. Presentation in this area is significant because it encourages learning at higher levels; that is, going beyond basic knowledge and into comprehension, application, synthesis and evaluation (Bloom's taxonomy). Intellectual preparation includes knowledge of the subject matter, but currently accepted teaching methods and information on adult education recognize that a teacher does not know everything, and students' ideas are important and help to facilitate learning. Therefore, student participant's stories and ideas are important and teachers should welcome them.

The final chapter summarizes the holistic approach and challenges teachers and leaders to examine themselves to determine if they are prepared holistically, to teach or lead people to Christ. It also expresses how teachers may be encouraged. This chapter ends with a summary of the handbook.

ORGANIZATION OF THE CHAPTERS

A holistic approach to teaching includes several levels of preparation. Scripture references support each of the components. Preparation steps and exercises allow readers to reflect on the discussions that follow. The exercises provide teachers and students with topics for reflection and consideration. At the end of each chapter, there are preparation steps, scripture references, and exercises for reflection and self-evaluation. Prospective teachers may write their reactions to the discussions questions, steps and exercises and later follow up for further reflection.

CHAPTER SUMMARY

This chapter began by reviewing spiritual gifts emphasizing the calling of teachers to educate adults in the Christian faith. It provided definitions of some terms used in the handbook and of teaching and learning in an adult context. A holistic approach to teaching and learning was introduced; this approach is one that emphasizes the importance of spiritual, emotional, physical and intellectual aspects of teaching and learning. The chapter ended with an outline of the organization of the handbook. The next chapter focuses on the spiritual preparation for teaching.

CHAPTER 2

Spiritual Preparation

The fruit of the spirit is love, joy, peace, patience, kindness, goodness, faithfulness, gentleness, self-control; against such things there is no law (Galatians 5: 22-23).

    In this chapter you will review:
    Evidence of God's presence
    Reliance on the Holy Spirit
    Scripture references
    Preparation steps
    Spiritual exercises

EVIDENCE OF GOD'S PRESENCE

Many wonders of the world, the galaxy, and the universe would suggest there is a Creator. Even lesser wonders of beauty and awe may provide similar experiences of God's presence. When one goes to the golf course, one may instantly remember the 23rd Psalm: "He makes me lie down in green pastures; He leads me beside quiet waters. He restores my soul" (v. 2-3). Natural beauty is serene and it reminds some people of God as their Creator and the Creator of the universe. For true Christians, nature is unequivocally God's creation and demonstrates His greatness. It reminds people that God is of a spiritual nature, and that those who worship Him must worship Him in Spirit and in truth (John 4:24). His first commandment is to worship Him (Deuteronomy 6). Since Christians ought to put God first in everything, spiritual preparation for service comes first.

This chapter provides a discussion on spiritual preparation for teaching. It begins with a calling of the Holy Spirit; God is calling or revealing His will for peoples' lives. Preparation steps and exercises for readers follow discussion sections.

Spiritual preparation is an essential component for readiness to teach the Christian faith. As such, teachers must consider prayerfully the impact they may have on peoples' lives. Teaching is a spiritual phenomenon since it involves a transformation or change in attitude, knowledge and behaviour. These changes affect the lives of some of the people called to teach or lead others to Christ. Some examples of change in peoples' lives follow.

SIGNS AND WONDERS

When Saul met Jesus on the way to Damascus (Acts 9:3-5), there was a spiritual awakening in a dramatic way. The bright light from heaven, the blindness, the vision, all contributed to the change in Saul's life. Once he realized that God had called him to share the gospel, it was easy to use his zealousness in a righteous manner. God lead Saul to understand that he was persecuting God's people, and that he should use his energy instead for praising God and teaching. After his miraculous conversion, God sent Ananias to help Saul prepare for teaching. God prepared Ananias to meet Saul. God also said to Ananias in a vision "Go, for he is a chosen instrument of Mine, to bear My name before the Gentiles and kings and the sons of Israel (Acts 9:15). This direct intervention is one way that God reveals Himself to people. Although people cannot see God or the Holy Spirit, some people can feel the presence of the Holy Spirit or experience the Holy Spirit through signs. There are many other examples in the Bible of people having an encounter with God.

Before Jesus came, people had direct and indirect contact with God. God spoke to Adam and Eve in the garden (Genesis 1). When Moses saw the burning bush, he knew that God was there. He heard the Lord's voice telling him that he was standing on holy ground, and he took off his shoes in obedience (Exodus 3:2-5).

Abraham was a righteous man who obeyed God's orders to prepare to sacrifice his only son. However, God provided a sacrificial lamb for him. Abraham heard a noise and a ram appeared from the bushes for a sacrifice. God provided a sacrifice so that Abraham would not have to sacrifice his son (Genesis 22:12-13).

Another righteous man, Zacharias, had a vision. An angel came to tell him that his prayers were answered and that he would have a son (Luke 1:13). You can imagine the joy this brought to Zacharias and his wife Elizabeth, as they so much wanted a child.

Angels announced the birth of Christ to the shepherds (Luke 2: 9-10). At the cross, darkness came on the earth (Mark 15:33). At Pentecost, there was an unfamiliar noise like rushing mighty wind (Acts 2:1-2). This is when God sent the Holy Sprit to walk alongside his people. Another sign at that time was that people who spoke in different languages could understand each other. God manifests Himself in many ways to ordinary people. People also see signs through answers to prayer. Answers are not always positive, yet this helps people to understand what God has in store for their lives.

Christians should look for evidence of the leading of the Holy Spirit around them and be ready to accept God's will. There is a well-known story of a drowning man who prayed to God for deliverance. God sent a lifeboat and a helicopter to save him but the man did not realize these would save him. As the story goes, these were saving devices, coming from God. The story continues that when the man died and went to heaven, God reminded him of His provision for saving the man. The drowning man had rejected them because he did not or could not see how God worked mysteriously to provide for him. God still uses signs in these days to show His people His presence, through answer to prayer and miracles or unexplained happenings in people's lives.

The Bible provides instruction regarding spiritual preparation. Teachers must prepare by searching the Bible for these instructions. First, they must accept salvation. "For by grace you have been saved through faith; and that not of yourselves, it is the gift of God; not as a result of works, so that no one may boast" (Ephesians 2:8-9). Next, they must discover or recognize their spiritual gift, as they are lead by the Holy Spirit. Teachers must also publicly acknowledge the Lordship of God as evidenced by their walk with God (Galatians 5:24). They should wholeheartedly depend on God.

RELIANCE ON GOD

The preceding stories show how God was always near to His people. Just as He provided for Abraham, He will provide for teachers. He gave Zacharias the desire of his heart. He taught Saul the right way and sent people to guide him. This is how the Holy Spirit will be with teachers. God will bring experiences in their lives that will prepare them spiritually for His work. The important thing to recognize is that there is a calling, a leading, and experiences that will prepare teachers spiritually for the work God has called them to do.

Although all people are sinners, Christians must rely on God to be with them always as they strive towards holiness. God knows everyone's weaknesses, and He will help teachers in these weaknesses. Like the psalmist in Psalm 139, 23-24, we can ask, "search me, O God, and know my heart, try me and know my anxious thoughts; and see if there be any hurtful way in me, and lead me in the everlasting way." Again recognizing we all are human; we must remember what Paul said to the Corinthians. He said, "No temptation has overtaken you but such as is common to man; and God is faithful, who will not allow you to be tempted beyond what you are able, but with the temptation will provide the way of escape also, so that you will be able to endure it" (1 Corinthians 10:13). With this in mind, people are to think of the fruit of the Holy Spirit.

Galatians 5:22-23 lists the fruit of the Spirit. The fruits of love, joy peace, patience, gentleness, and so on are essential attributes teachers need to emulate if they want to teach God's word. The fruit helps not only to increase spiritual strength, but also to act as a code of behaviour for Christian living. The fruit of the Spirit act as a standard or benchmark for maturing Christians. Aspiring to attain these qualities, and then apply them, will help teachers to prepare spiritually for service.

SCRIPTURE REFERENCE

Before Jesus left the earth, He made a promise that He would not leave His people alone or comfortless, so He sent His Holy Spirit to walk alongside them. This promise provides comfort because God's people can rely on the leading of the Holy Spirit. Jesus said to his disciples:

> But the Helper, the Holy Spirit, whom the father will send in My name, He will teach you all things, and

bring to your remembrance all that I said to you. (John 14:26)

We see this promise fulfilled at Pentecost when the Holy Spirit filled believers as evidenced by their immediate reactions. Of course, they acted and thought differently from those who did not receive the Holy Spirit. The disciple Luke was there and provided this account:

> Peter said to them, "Repent, and each of you be baptized in the name of Jesus Christ for the forgiveness of your sins; and you will receive the gift of the Holy Spirit." (Acts 2: 38)

Many Christians have accepted the leadership of the Holy Spirit. When teachers accept the Holy Spirit, Jesus will be with them all the time and His Holy Spirit will lead them in their teaching.

Paul, the apostle, explained that the fruit of the Spirit would lead God's people into all truths. Paul instructed Timothy to be, "strong in the grace that is in Christ Jesus" (2 Timothy 2:1) and also to, "be diligent to present yourself approved of God as a workman who does not need to be ashamed, handling accurately the word of truth" (v. 15). Christians are to, "flee from youthful lusts and pursue righteousness, faith, love and peace" (v. 22).

In preparing Timothy for ministry, Paul, the apostle, clearly explained to him the type of people God chooses to do His work. In his epistle to Timothy, he said, "You therefore, my son, be strong in the grace that is in Christ Jesus. The things which you have heard from me in the presence of many witnesses, **entrust these to faithful men who will be able to teach others also."** (2 Tim 2:1-2) Later in his letter to Timothy, he said,

> Preach the word; be ready in season and out of season; reprove, rebuke, exhort, with great patience and instruction. For the time will come when they will not endure sound doctrine (2 Tim 4:2-3).

Paul instructed Timothy. The disciples were instructed in Acts 6:4 "to devote ourselves to prayer and to the ministry of the word." Other people may have different jobs in ministry. In Acts 6:3 they were told to "select from among you seven men of good reputation, full of the Spirit and of wisdom" to put in charge of another task, which was to serve tables.

The Holy Bible provides sound doctrine, and although Bible scholars expound on it, one must not hesitate to return to the original source and understand the context of the doctrine. As teachers look to the Bible for spiritual guidance, they need to examine themselves. Do you remember the proverbial dog that looked into the water and saw his shadow? This dog thought he saw another dog. As believers we must understand that not only we are looking at our own reflection in the water, but others will also observe our reflection in the water. Our image must reflect authenticity, and our light must shine. Here are some preparation steps that will assist you in seeking the work of the Holy Spirit. These steps can be taken in any order.

SCRIPTURE PREPARATION STEPS

1. Pray for guidance and leading by the Holy Spirit.
2. Confirm and affirm your calling to teach (1 Corinthians 12:14-18 and Ephesians 4:12-14).
3. Prepare your heart for knowledge and understanding of the scriptures (Philippians 4:8, Romans 8:5-8, Proverbs 6:16-20).
4. Ask God to remove those things that are not spiritual from your mind (Colossians 3:8).
5. Pray for the fruit of the spirit to be working in you, (Colossians 3:12).
    These preparation steps are necessary for God's people, especially for those who have received the calling to teach God's Word. The exercises below will help with application of this section.

SPIRITUAL EXERCISE

1. Write your inspirational verse here, a verse that helped you to recognize your spiritual gift or calling to teach or lead others to Jesus Christ. You may add any significant sign that marked the moment of your discovery. _____
   _____
   _____
   _____
   _____
   _____

2. List specific needs you want to pray for regarding your spiritual preparation. These may include a prayer for the leading of the Holy Spirit. _____
   _____
   _____
   _____
   _____
   _____
   _____

3. Reflect on your first teaching or leading assignment (not necessarily formal teaching) and list the spiritual concerns you remember having. Try to remember what specifically caused those concerns, and write this down. Think of and reflect on a verse of scripture that will help you in this area and make a note of it.
   _____
   _____
   _____
   _____
   _____

4. Consider steps you need to take to improve yourself spiritually. Changes in attitude may be noteworthy; for example, listening, obeying, and applying yourself spiritually with an attitude of love, acceptance, obedience, peace, and gentleness.

___

5. Write a short prayer that will remind you that you are God's instrument for sharing the gospel with others, and that you are depending on Him for guidance.

___

CHAPTER SUMMARY

This chapter focused on spiritual preparation. Every teacher must prepare himself or herself to be holy and acceptable to God by accepting the gift of salvation and concentrating on and applying the fruit of the Spirit in his or her life. Letting go of those things that are an abomination to God will leave room for accommodating the love, joy, peace, and patience that teachers need to be able to lead others in understanding God's work and His will for their lives and in the lives of other people. Spiritual preparation is a very serious matter. Christians must allow the Holy Spirit to help them search their hearts and prepare them for teaching or serving in other ministries. We need to remember that teaching is a special calling and preparation for it is essential. The next chapter deals with emotional preparation for teaching and leading.

CHAPTER 3

Emotional Preparation

So, as those who have been chosen of God, holy and beloved, put on a heart of compassion, kindness, humility, gentleness and patience. (Colossians 3:12)

This chapter focuses on emotional preparation for teaching, specifically:

    The greatest commandment
    Building trust
    Knowing your audience
    Dealing with feelings
    Scripture references
    Emotional, intuitive and relational preparation steps
    Emotional exercise

EMOTIONS

Most people feed on positive thoughts and kind words that stimulate emotions. These thoughts light up their lives and help them proceed confidently. Negative emotions on the other hand can be devastating and may even lead to depression. Here is a simple story of how positive actions lighted up the lives in one family.

It was at a 25th wedding anniversary reception when parents telephoned to wish their daughter and son-in-law a happy anniversary. The first words uttered by the father were, "Is everybody happy?" The siblings who were listening to the conversation yelled, "Yes," with joy. That question had a special meaning to this family. That father used to ask this question several times when his children were young. Usually when he arrived home from work, he would open his front door and those words would be the announcement of his arrival home. His children would run to the door and he would take them in his arms. They would be overjoyed especially if he brought them a special treat. That action instigated an emotional experience, which always surfaced and reminded his children of happy times. Intuitively, they felt loved and accepted. They remembered the great stories he told and their special loving times as children. Stories may relate to experiences and emotions which if shared can enhance teaching. The previous chapter dealt with spiritual preparation, this chapter discusses how Christians can prepare emotionally for teaching.

This chapter focuses on emotional preparation needed for teaching generally and, especially teaching of the Christian faith.

It encourages building loving relationships with those around us, especially our students. It reminds teachers of the greatest commandment, which is to love the Lord our God with all our heart, and second, to love our neighbour as we love ourselves (see Matthew 22:37-39; also see Deuteronomy chapters five and six). This chapter also discusses how building trust and knowing your audience facilitates learning. Scripture references, preparation steps and exercises are included to reinforce the need to be emotionally prepared. When we speak of emotions, we refer to feelings. Feeling good about yourself facilitates preparing emotionally and intuitively, and puts your students in a frame of mind conducive to learning. Feelings of love, joy, peace, gentleness, and patience help teachers and learners. Jesus commanded that we love one another.

THE GREATEST COMMANDMENT

While Jesus was on earth, one of the Pharisees, a lawyer, asked Jesus, which was the greatest commandment. Jesus said:

> You shall love the Lord your God with all your heart, and with all your soul, and with all your mind. This is the great and foremost commandment. The second is like it, 'You shall love your neighbour as yourself.'. (Mathew 22:37-39)

John the disciple reminded us of how we should love God and each other. He writes of Jesus teaching them, saying, "this is My commandment, that you love one another, just as I have loved you." (John 15:12) When we obey this commandment, we put God first in our lives and in everything that we do.

One may summarize The Ten Commandments in Deuteronomy chapter five into one important commandment of love. If we truly love, we will not break any of the other commandments. A loving disposition creates an atmosphere that is conducive to learning. It incorporates kindness, empathy, understanding others, sharing, giving, and caring, which students will intuitively feel as love and acceptance. Jesus exemplified all these characteristics by caring physically and understanding people's needs, physical and emotional as well as spiritual and intellectual, as He walked on earth performing miracles, telling stories, and teaching people. These characteristics are embodiments of the small word "love." Love is a requirement for good relationships to work better, and to improve bad relationships. First Corinthians 13: 4-8 elaborates the intricacies of love. Many pastors and others recite this passage at weddings as they admonish young couples. Teachers also must show love as they teach and prepare themselves emotionally, intuitively, and relationally.

Preparing emotionally

Emotional preparation starts with looking inward at feelings and examining your intuitive state of mind. People react intuitively to their emotions. Here is an example of intuitiveness. A child crawled under a bench in church one Sunday morning and looked back to see if her mother was watching. The mother and child's eyes met and the child could tell what was in the mother's mind. That expression told the child that the mother disapproved of the behaviour, and the child could expect some discipline when the service was over. Even as the child understood that expression on her mother's face, so too teachers can observe their students' facial expressions and perceive what those expressions are trying to convey. The look on students' faces may express utter enjoyment, concern, or confusion. Teachers need to observe students' body language, interpret it, and respond to the students intuitively, questioningly, or otherwise, to find the mood of the class or of a particular student. Once teachers perceive the mood of participants, they may relate or react appropriately to make the students feel more comfortable as the situation allows. These observations will help teachers better understand students and decide how they should relate to them.

Additionally, a teacher can present a pleasant disposition, a smile, and a welcoming demeanour to help make student participants feel relaxed and ready for learning. The atmosphere should be non-threatening. Teachers can create this atmosphere by building trust.

BUILDING TRUST

A good teacher-student relationship is essential in learning, as it encourages a positive connection from which trust can be built. A climate of trust is essential to a good learning climate. If a teacher appears genuine, shows empathy and acceptance, the relationship between the students and the teacher will likely be positive and trusting. Griffin (1993) suggests building trust is more important than technical teaching skills and scholarly knowledge. Technical knowledge is very valuable, but even more so, the teacher must reach out to students and follow through on his or her intuition. A teacher may sense that the student wants to talk to him or her privately, or that a student may be hurting in some way. Reaching out is therefore a key ingredient in building trust and facilitating the learning process.

One cannot separate teaching from learning. If learning and teaching are corroborative, both the learner and the teacher will be more satisfied working together as co-learners, where the teacher requests the sharing of experiences of the learner. Participants come to class with different experiences and backgrounds. As human beings, students and teachers alike are subject to temptations every day. Being human, they come to class with fear, worry and anxiety about the problems in the world. They love, hurt, feel pain and experience joy. As people experience the feelings of joy, sadness, apprehension, love, anxiety, and fear, they need to put on the whole amour of God (Ephesians 6:11) to help them deal with these feelings. If they could share their experiences in class, this would enrich learning. This sharing encourages co-operation and participation and reinforces the teacher/student relationship. This sharing may also build trust. One component for building trust is to know your audience so that you may empathize and relate to them.

KNOW YOUR AUDIENCE

Participants in your class may be young adults, young couples, parents of young children, parents with adolescent children, or empty nesters. People have different needs, backgrounds, education, goals, expectations, and interests. They all have life experiences that continue to mould them into the unique persons they are. Normally a person needs others to know and accept him or her. Participants' names are important to them, therefore teachers need to learn names of students as soon as possible. Each person is unique: gender, health, and social status. Each brings a different perspective to the class. Knowing the educational background will help in the level of delivery of content. Teachers should ensure that they meet certain class expectations and pay attention to cultural differences. Some participants may need extrinsic rewards to motivate them. Other students are intrinsically motivated without rewards. These aspects need consideration and must be kept in mind as a teacher plans the curriculum, the actual content to be taught, the delivery methods, goals and objectives of the lesson, and an evaluation to determine whether their goals were accomplished. Teachers have to be prepared to deal with these differences and address specific needs of individual students.

Favers and Kerssen (2002) compare people in a class to the seven dwarves in "Snow White." If the seven dwarves were in your class, Dopey would be pleasant and supportive; Grumpy would be cynical and intelligent but difficult to please; Sneezy would be fragile and perhaps afraid to participate; Bashful would not stick around to ask additional questions; Sleepy would be bored and want to leave early, while Doc would be assertive and a problem solver. People are so different, and it would help if teachers knew about their students' needs and wants, their likes and dislikes as they relate to learning. We do not have to look very far to see that we come in many different shapes and colours. We come from many backgrounds and cultures; we think differently and we learn differently. These differences may be spiritual, cultural, emotional, physical, and intellectual.

David Keirsey (1998) in his book *Please Understand Me* puts it this way:

People are different in fundamental ways. They want different things; they have different motives, purposes, aims, values, needs, drives, impulses and urges... They think differently, perceive, understand, comprehend and cognize differently.

As human beings, people are subject to temptations everyday. Being human, we worry and are anxious, are scared and have to think about the cares of this world. Since we are so different, we react to circumstances in different ways. Teachers need to recognize those differences and act accordingly.

DEALING WITH FEELINGS

Here is how some Bible characters dealt with feelings. Saul was passionately persecuting the saints until he met God on the way to Damascus. Then he was "sore afraid" (Acts 9), so terribly frightened. So were the shepherds when they saw the angel who announced the birth of Christ (Luke 2:9). Jesus wept when Lazarus died (John 11:35). All people share emotions like fear, sorrow, zeal, love, anger, and joy.

Experiences throughout the weeks, years, lifetimes, leave an impression on people's minds. The September 11, 2001 disaster was one of those experiences that leave an indelible impression on people's minds. Some people reacted to this disaster with sadness, disbelief, anger, or other emotions. Disasters like fire or flood or death bring about other emotions. Expressions people hear at work, and even at home as they listen to the television, have an effect on their thinking and their reactions. As they experience these feelings of joy, of sadness, of apprehension, of love, of anxiety, and of fear, they must try "to put on the full armour of God" (Ephesians 6:11), as this will help them to deal with problems. Teachers must pray for wisdom to understand students' emotions. Remember, God is love, and He will help teachers to prepare themselves for dealing with emotions.

Emotions are sometimes positive and sometimes negative. Body language is a good indicator of a person's emotional state. A customer service attendant may be cheerful or grumpy and clients sense this disposition intuitively. Parents who scream at children reveal a state of emotional distress. Those people who are seen laughing, hugging, and reaching out to others make a statement of emotional wellbeing which some may interpret as a positive outlook on life. Sometimes people can see an expression of disappointment on others' faces. Focusing on the fruit of the spirit (Galatians 5:22-23) may counter some negative emotions. This passage is a good reminder of positive emotions.

Integrating emotional and spiritual capabilities reminds Christians to look to the Holy Spirit for God's guidance. Openness and sharing will show student participants that they are not alone and will encourage them to share their joys and sorrows. Teachers can share their emotions, but they must be careful with what they share and avoid being too personal. Balance is the key. Teachers should look to God for guidance in deciding what they should share with others, and what they should leave entirely at His throne. As much as teachers have to show compassion, they need the Lord's compassion as well.

SCRIPTURE REFERENCES

Paul said, "Put on a heart of compassion, kindness, humility, gentleness and patience" (Colossians 3:12). These virtues will enhance teaching and make students feel comfortable. Teachers also need to feel comfortable. Teachers may be very apprehensive at the beginning of their teaching career, and feel very sensitive to students' comments. The Lord Jesus Christ knows teachers' needs and will provide compassion and encouragement. Remember:

> The Lord's loving kindnesses indeed never cease, for His compassions never fail. They are new every morning; Great is your faithfulness. (Lamentations 3:22-23)

Jesus showed compassion:

> Seeing the people, He felt compassion for them, because they were distressed and dispirited like sheep without a shepherd. Then He said to His disciples, "The harvest is plentiful, but the workers are few. (Matthew 9:36-37)

As teachers deal with emotions, they are encouraged to:

> Let your speech always be with grace, as though seasoned with salt, so that you will know how you should respond to each person. (Colossians 4:6)

In writing to the early church in the book of Hebrews, Peter stressed growth and maturity. In chapter twelve he used feeding as a metaphor to explain that babies must eat crushed and softened food, while mature people can chew so therefore they can eat solid food. Teaching young Christians requires a breakdown of advanced concepts into simple parts. Peter was concerned because some people were not learning as fast as they could. Consider the following passage:

> For though by this time you ought to be teachers, you have need again for someone to teach you the elementary principles of the oracles of God, and you have come to need milk and not solid food. But solid food is for the mature, who because of practice have their senses trained to discern good and evil (Hebrews 5:12,14).

It takes time to learn, but a heart of love and encouragement can accomplish great things.

> Since you have in obedience to the truth purified your souls for a sincere love of the brethren, fervently love one another from the heart (1 Peter 1:22).

The Lord knows that workers are needed in the field and will prepare His workers. Paul encouraged the church in Rome: "be devoted to one another in brotherly love; give preference to one another in honour (Romans 12:10). Teachers need to love and provide encouragement, and again;

> Be kind to one another, tender-hearted, forgiving each other, just as God in Christ also has forgiven you. (Ephesians 4:32)

Griffin (1993, p.12) offers some suggestions for teachers to follow when dealing with students' emotional needs. Griffin refers to the subconscious mind, which interacts with experience to make sense of learning. The combination of relational, emotional and intuitive experience will create a synergy and will lift learning to a higher level. Some of Griffin's suggestions are in the emotional preparation steps shown below:

EMOTIONAL PREPARATION STEPS

1. Think about talking with students (this may help someone sort out his or her emotions)
2. Consider how you will support and provide encouragement to your students or learners.
3. Find someone whom you trust and respect, but who thinks differently about a topic. Try to understand and sympathize with that person's point of view. This may help you to understand yourself and move you towards clarity and understanding of others.
4. Prepare your heart for caring and nurturing students.

Teachers are like everyone else. They are not perfect but they should examine themselves to see if they are bearing most of the fruit expected of those who strive to be emotionally pure. Here are some exercises that will help you evaluate your emotional state.

EMOTIONAL EXERCISE

1. How are you prepared to share your state of emotional health? Are you prepared to become vulnerable and open so that your audience will understand you, and so that you will feel they trust enough to share their emotional state with you? _____
   _____
   _____
   _____
   _____
   _____

2. List some positive attitudes. Make an effort to emulate these positive attitudes so that you can help your students and enhance your teaching. _____
   _____
   _____
   _____
   _____
   _____

3. How do you plan to pass on positive emotions to the participants in your class? _____
   _____
   _____
   _____
   _____
   _____

4. Think of a situation where you may want to give encouragement. Explain how you would plan to do this. _____
   _____

Preparing to Teach God's Word

5. Are there any negative emotions that will take away from your teaching? Have you prayed about this? Try to correct them before class begins. It may be a situation you could use as a good example to change an attitude and to build trust. _____

6. What are the telling signs (body language) that give away your state of emotional health and add or take away from your teaching? (Colossians 3:8) and (Proverbs. 6:16-19) _____

7. Write a short payer for your emotional guidance. _____

CHAPTER SUMMARY

Emotional preparation includes embracing compassion and showing empathy for student participants. Knowing your audience and understanding their needs, backgrounds, culture, education, and expectations could help a teacher to decide what action to take to help students feel emotionally comfortable and to build trust. Teachers must build trust so that there may be open and honest relationships. Private discussions may help to build better relationships between teachers and students. Building relationships is a key to facilitating learning, especially when trying to influence change in attitudes and values.

Some changes in attitudes and values are external and teachers may be able to observe them physically; others are internal and one cannot observe them. Teachers must be prepared to facilitate change in an environment that is conducive to learning. The next chapter addresses the learning environment and physical preparation. These attributes will also enhance teaching and learning.

CHAPTER 4

Physical Preparation

Run in such a way that you may win. Everyone who competes in the games exercises self-control in all things...Therefore I run in such a way, as not without aim; I box in such a way, as not beating for the air; but I discipline my body and make it my slave... (1 Corinthians 9:24-27)

This chapter discusses physical needs and includes:

    Running the race
    Physical fitness
    Environmental needs
    Scripture references
    Physical preparation steps
    Physical exercises

Continuing with the holistic approach and the proverbial strings of spiritual and emotional considerations, teachers must embrace physical preparation. The physical environment must be conducive to how adults learn, as adults, oftentimes more than children, need to be comfortable in order to learn. You may have seen young children lying in the foetal position, kneeling on chairs, or standing beside a table to paint, write or color in their workbooks, even if desks are available. They adopt a comfortable position that meets their immediate needs. Being a good teacher of adults means understanding how to also make them feel comfortable while learning.

As an example, families with athletic children expect to have a very high food bill. This is because people who train ardently for their sport need energy for the mental and physical rigor they must endure to do well. They must prepare mentally and physically for each game day, especially during playoffs, national and international events. It takes discipline to maintain physical fitness and develop physical strength. Christians too need physical strength. Thank God we do not go through life alone; we can pray for health, strength, and endurance to finish the game of life and win the prize. When it is over, we can say "well done" and feel very satisfied that all the effort, sacrifice, and discipline paid off in the end.

This chapter addresses the physical stamina and the physical environment in which adults prefer to learn. It discusses the need to prepare physically for teaching God's word and begins with the teacher's physical state of body and mind. Then follows a description of the physical environment that is conducive to learning. This description addresses physical concerns and includes scripture references, preparation steps, and preparation exercises.

RUNNING THE RACE

Just like people who run marathons to raise funds for cancer, diabetes, or multiple sclerosis, teachers also are running for a cause. In this type of competition, all who run are winners. Each is concerned about contributing to that cause, and most succeed in making that contribution according to his or her ability. Each donation increases the overall effort and is meaningful. All teachers make a difference in reaching others for Christ.

The apostle Paul likened his walk with the Lord as being in a race (1 Corinthians 9:24-25). He presented this picture to show how disciplined a person must be if they want to win their race. He had a goal not to be an "also ran" because he wanted to win. To run this metaphoric race, those who teach the Christian faith follow a course of disciplined behaviour to prepare for the course. In a teaching context, this means not only to be prepared physically but also to prepare the environment where teaching and learning must take place.

The book of Acts describes how early Christians worshiped in homes as well as in synagogues. Home worship optimized the comfort of the home where sharing and communication would be easier and true fellowship more natural without the formal sophistication of the temple. Teachers must therefore engage themselves in physical preparation as they consider the environment where their teaching will take place.

ENVIRONMENTAL PREPARATION

Knowles (1980), a respected leader in adult education, explained the learning climate, physical and psychological, should be carefully constructed for acceptance, respect, and support. He acknowledged that this will encourage a desire to learn, and learners will be involved with the process. The environment includes the classroom or meeting place, proper lighting, acoustics, temperature and resources for adults. These are important considerations when deciding on how to make adults feel comfortable and ready for learning. Physical concerns and their effects on learning also include uses of the senses, hearing, seeing, feeling, and smelling. The smell of coffee or hot chocolate on a cold day, or the sight of a pitcher of lemonade on a hot day is not only inviting but appeals to the senses of sight and smell.

Environmental preparation includes comfortable seating that is arranged to accommodate adult learning. Placing chairs in a horseshoe formation or circle will enhance adult learning. This arrangement encourages open communication and facilitates dialogue among participants and teacher. It involves the teacher as part of the learning group. To facilitate open communication in the class, teachers should present themselves as learners who are willing to accept the experiences of the audience. Adults love to participate on an equal basis. They have a lot to contribute because of their many and varied life experiences. Their experiences could increase understanding and help others to relate to the subject or content being taught or discussed.

Writers of adult education literature suggest other variables of environmental factors that influence adult learning. Learning resources are imperative and need special consideration. These may include handouts in large print and brighter colors to facilitate reading. If there is a chalkboard, use red or bright colour chalk, as this is easier on aging eyes. Soft comfortable chairs are important as this increases comfort and in turn, cognition. These comforts may reduce back pain and sore backsides. If possible, provide a table to support and encourage writing. Speak loud enough to ensure audibility. This accommodates older adults and helps to hold their interest. Be enthusiastic enough so no one falls asleep. Involve the audience as much as possible. Allow them to share their stories.

PHYSICAL CONCERNS

In addition to environmental preparation, teachers and facilitators must consider being in good physical condition as they share with participants. This does not necessarily mean physique, but rather alludes to a heightened level of enthusiasm and energy. A teacher or facilitator needs to be exuberant and exciting in class. If they are rested and well-nourished, enthusiasm may follow and student participation and interests are likely to increase as discussion increases. A hungry, half-hearted person will not make a good impression on the students. Get enough rest and eat properly so that you will be energized, eager and full of the passion required for providing interest in the topic you present. Also, consider your attire as appropriate enough to gain the respect of the audience.

Dressing appropriately for the occasion makes some students feel comfortable and perhaps more respectful to the teacher and the content being taught. For older adults, proper grooming is important. While younger adults may appreciate a facilitator who dresses more like them, older adults may prefer to see their leader/facilitator modestly dressed. However, dressing appropriately for young adults does not mean going to extremes. The following story illustrates some behavioural concerns.

There is a story of a grandmother who gave a lesson to her granddaughter. The granddaughter thought that because she was young, she could dress inappropriately, by that meaning, topless. She told her grandmother that she was only showing her "rose buds." One day before friends arrived to visit the granddaughter, the grandmother appeared topless in the living room. The granddaughter was horrified and embarrassed that her grandmother would do this and asked for an explanation. The grandmother told her granddaughter that she could show her "hanging baskets." The granddaughter was not at all impressed with the grandmother's explanation but she did get the point of this action. Appropriate attire for activities and occasions will help students to feel comfortable and even reduce anxiety among students. Another topic related to student anxiety is the stress level of the teacher.

Although stress is a fact in our daily lives, a teacher must try not to appear to be stressed or burnt out. If teachers follow a simple exercise program, this will help them to reduce stress levels. Simple stretches may help to release some tension. Listening to classical music may also induce calmness and peace and reduce stress. Just as the ten virgins prepared themselves for the bridegroom, so teachers must prepare for their teaching. They had their lamps trimmed and ready. (Parable of Ten Virgins, Matthew 25:1-13). Remember to trim your lamps and keep them burning, as the fuel must be available for the light to shine brightly.

SCRIPTURE REFERENCE

Running to win involves conditioning for the long haul. Christians may condition themselves through daily prayer. Daily praying and preparing is imperative. God will prepare His people and make them confident for their race. The scriptures provide words of comfort and confidence. For example, Paul confirmed this when he wrote to Timothy:

> For God has not given us a spirit of timidity, but of power and love and discipline (2 Timothy 1:7)

Teachers are to accept God's love and the power He promised to His leaders. This power will help teachers with the discipline they need to keep conditioning themselves as leaders.

In his writings to the Romans, Paul reminded them about their bodies. He instructed them to take care of their bodies physically as well as spiritually. Scripture confirms that the body is the temple of the Lord.

> Therefore I urge you, brethren, by the mercies of God, to present your bodies a living and holy sacrifice, acceptable to God, which is your spiritual service of worship. (Romans 12:1)

As human beings, we do get old and weak, but age should not reduce the focus of our race. When Moses was old and "no longer able to come and go, " (Deuteronomy 31: 2), he gave this advice to the children of Israel:

> Be strong and courageous, do not be afraid or tremble at them, for the Lord your God is the one who goes with you. He will not fail you or forsake you. (Deuteronomy 31:6)

The Lord will increase our physical strength and be with us. We can depend on Him to renew our strength as we continue our race as long as we can.

> Do you not know that you are a temple of God and that the spirit of God dwells in you? (1 Corinthians 3:16)

The following preparation steps will assist teachers in finishing the good race of teaching in high standing.

PHYSICAL PREPARATION STEPS

If we accept the coaching and training of the Holy Spirit and God's Word, the race will appear to be easy. The following steps are reminders that environmental preparation and physical conditioning are important for running the metaphoric race and finishing the course.

1. Consider classroom layout for maximum comfort and participation.
2. Prepare a list of supplies needed for the session
3. Organize for adequate lighting and comfortable temperature.
4. Arrange for audio equipment and such details as necessary if available.

5. Arrange for snack and a break.
6. Request a volunteer to help with environmental preparation. This will leave you with more time to concentrate on the lesson plan and presentation (discussed in the next chapter).

These considerations are important for adults and are conducive to learning. The following exercises will help determine if we have adequately prepared the physical environment for learning.

PHYSICAL EXERCISE

1. Draw a picture or describe the layout of your classroom, including positioning of presentation aids. _____
   _____
   _____
   _____
   _____
   _____
   _____

2. Make a list of the supplies you need to enhance your teaching.
   _____
   _____
   _____
   _____
   _____
   _____

3. Consider the number of volunteers you need to assists in non-instructional activities. How will you go about selecting them?
   _____
   _____
   _____
   _____
   _____
   _____

Preparing to Teach God's Word

4. List some non-instructional activities to be planned (e.g. snack or coffee arrangements). _____
   _____
   _____
   _____
   _____
   _____

5. How will you accommodate adults with hearing or other physical challenges? _____
   _____
   _____
   _____
   _____
   _____

6. List some ways to consistently maintain your energy level.
   _____
   _____
   _____
   _____
   _____

7. Write a prayer to remind you to be prepared physically, to prepare the environment, and to attend to the physical needs of participants in your class. _____
   _____
   _____
   _____
   _____
   _____

8. What attitudes do you think will help you to increase strength, power, confidence and courage, and reduce timidity and fear?

_____
_____
_____
_____
_____
_____

CHAPTER SUMMARY

Physical preparation includes environmental preparation and attending to the physical concerns of the teacher and students. Environmental preparation takes into account classroom layout, selection of supplies and other resources, and students' comfort, including temperature, seating arrangements, and audio-visual aids. Physical preparation considers appropriate attire, a high level of energy, enthusiasm, and excitement about the topic being taught. Advance preparation and organization allows teachers to accommodate adult students, including students with physical challenges. A relaxed atmosphere is non-threatening and essential for maximizing learning and encouraging class participation.

Whereas this chapter focused on physical preparation, the next chapter addresses intellectual preparation for maximizing learning.

CHAPTER 5

Intellectual Preparation

But the goal of our instruction is love from a pure heart and a good conscience and a sincere faith. For some men, straying from these things, have turned aside to fruitless discussion, wanting to be teachers of the Law, even though they do not understand either what they are saying or the matters about which they make confident assertions (1 Timothy 1:5-7).

This chapter will focus on:

- Learning and teaching
- Adult education
- Learning styles
- Learning activities
- Learning objectives
- Delivery methods and presentation
- Using technology
- Student evaluation
- Teacher evaluation
- Content
- Scripture references
- Intellectual steps
- Intellectual exercises

In previous chapters there were discussions on spiritual preparation, emotional preparation, and physical preparation. This chapter introduces teaching strategies and preparation for delivering scriptural material. The chapter provides more information on adult education, learning styles, learning activities, learning objectives, teaching methods, delivery, and evaluation. It includes some teaching tips that may strengthen teaching skills and facilitate learning. Integrating spiritual and emotional preparation, coupled with physical and intellectual preparation, are some components of a teaching strategy. The result is a holistic approach to preparing to teach or lead a Bible study. What we teach is just as important as how we teach. Although this handbook does not focus on curriculum or content, knowledge of topics or subjects taught is very necessary. These sections will lay a foundation for good teaching. To begin, a story will help to illustrate how lack of important information can mislead people.

Have you noticed that some people like to speak convincingly about topics of which they have almost no knowledge? Someone once asked for directions to a certain place, and the respondent, who did not know the destination, was adamant in providing directions to the lost traveler. Some arrogant persons like this one are afraid to admit their ignorance in certain areas and therefore mislead others. Thank God that the majority of people are not that way and would simply say, "I don't know," and would then be smart enough to direct the inquirer to a knowledgeable source. To be prepared for teaching, one needs to have the knowledge base of content and the andragogical and leadership skills for teaching. Andragogy is the study of how adults learn and this knowledge is very useful for those who teach adults. This knowledge is perhaps what most readers were anticipating in this handbook. To understand teaching one must also understand learning. Integrating learning and teaching skills and preferences will enhance the gift or calling to teach.

LEARNING AND TEACHING

Learning is so complicated that educators are still trying to discover more of its intricacies. Humans are complex beings and therefore their learning is complex. People's bodies are comprised of many interrelated parts that work together to make sense of learning. These parts include not just physical but mental, spiritual, and intellectual aspects of learning. This chapter addresses learning and understanding at various levels. Bloom (1956) provides a taxonomy emphasizing various levels of learning. It begins with the basic knowledge level and moves to levels of comprehension, analysis, synthesis, and then evaluation. Knowledge of the levels of learning coupled with knowledge of learners' ability and preferences will inform teachers of individual differences and help them in planning. It is a good starting point for planning a teaching strategy. If teachers can understand these vital learning levels, their teaching will most likely improve.

Teaching

Everyone is involved in teaching at some time in his or her life. Each time a person tries to explain, to explore, to build or to manipulate something, that person is involved in teaching. Parents in particular are teachers. They begin teaching their infants by their actions and reactions and responses to their babies' cries. As children grow older, some follow the examples of their parents. Parents teach by example as they model behaviour, and encourage or discourage attitudes with positive or negative reinforcement. Those people who have children understand that it is a continuous process, one that can be very rewarding; yet it can be very frustrating at times. Just as parents may need help, so teachers may appreciate any tools they can use to facilitate learning. As parents teach through example, so Bible teachers can emulate the examples of those great leaders the heavenly Father has sent through the ages to guide people along life's way. The greatest example of all is our Lord and Saviour Jesus Christ. Jesus taught simply through examples, questioning, and using stories and allegories that appealed to a person's whole existence. His listeners could relate His stories to their life experiences. His examples included emphasizing spiritual and emotional needs, and caring physically for the sick. He was concerned about caring for body and soul.

Faust (1998) referred to caring as a relational teaching model that "provides a way to be deeply theological and dynamically effective in transforming the learner" (p. 1). He described this model as providing "a caring context where participation, growth, transformation and insight occur for the teacher and the learner when they risk sharing their critical reflections on issues." Using this relational model will encourage reflection and internal dialogue on issues. It should stimulate free expression of these issues in a caring environment. If applied properly, learning follows. Teachers must engage in meaningful dialogue with student participants and encourage reflection as learning takes place.

Learning

Educators describe learning as a change in behaviour, knowledge, skills, attitudes, and values. Those who teach the Christian faith propose to pass on Christian behaviour, knowledge, values, and attitudes to learners. Teachers need to understand the way adults learn to help them initiate change in their behaviour. Mezirow (1990), in writing about adult learners, explained, "Learning may be defined as the process of making a new or revised interpretation of the meaning of an experience which guides subsequent understanding, appreciation and action," (p.1). A revised interpretation of values or experiences may initiate a change in behaviour.

The systematic design of instruction may also help to accomplish this change. Since adult Christian students are most likely interested in Christian values, Christian educators must pay attention to these audiences as participants in their classes. These audiences are people from different backgrounds and with different personalities and experiences as explained in chapter four. Some people may be pleasant and ready, some cynical and apprehensive, some introverts, some extroverts.

People learn differently. Most people use all of their being to learn. Some people use all their senses, others use eyes more than ears, others need to use their hands, but all humans use their senses in some manner to enhance learning. Some will participate verbally while others may be good listeners. Preparing to teach involves more than understanding learners' preferences; teachers must consider planning in other areas.

Adult Education

Since this handbook is about teaching adult classes, it is mandatory to define adult education and the learning styles and delivery methods conducive to adult learning. Patricia Cranton (1989) in *Planning Instruction for Adult Learners*, defined adult education this way:

> Adult education is defined as any organized, sustained activity engaged in by adult individuals for the purpose of changing their knowledge, skills or values in any area (p. 4).

Adults can learn any subject. Experts in adult education say that given the appropriate time, adults will learn. It will take a teacher with knowledge of the methods by which adults learn to facilitate learning. Teachers as adult educators are not all the same. Each will have a personal philosophy and need to develop their personal theory of teaching. Principles of adult education are essential for understanding one's own theory of practice "and becoming aware of one's own beliefs" (Cranton 1997, p. 208 in *Working With Adult Learners*). A theory of practice is "simply a set of assumptions, beliefs and values about education" (Cranton 1997, p. 208). Some teaching principles developed by leaders in the field of adult education can help in identifying teachers' values and thus their theory. Personalities and past teaching experiences, including cultural values, are influences that affect teachers' theories of teaching and learning. The social environment also influences teachers' way of thinking. Some teachers see themselves as learners alongside their student participants. Others may see themselves as experts in their fields, and thus as providers of knowledge. Some teachers see themselves at some midway point between these two poles, depending on what they are trying to teach.

How teachers picture themselves will affect the way they teach. Each individual will have to adopt a teaching style in line with his or her orientation to teaching principles. Some principles include having adults actually participate in learning, giving them a choice in the delivery method. Incorporating past experiences and relying on them gives participants the opportunity to learn in different ways. Some participants may be intrinsically rewarded by the simple joy of learning, while others may need extrinsic rewards. Teachers may use extrinsic rewards for completing assignments, learning memory verses and reading and providing different perspectives. Children seem to need more extrinsic rewards than adults, whose need for life-long learning may be enough to motivate them. Adults want to learn for different reasons and they learn in many different ways. The following discussion explains some differences in the learning styles of adults and children.

Andragogy vs. Pedagogy

Children are different from adults, and they think, learn, and comprehend differently too. Pedagogical techniques are strategies that may help those who teach children. Andragogy is a new body of knowledge now emerging in the area of adult education. It focuses on how adults prefer to learn. Adult educators believe that adults like discussion, problem-solving, group work, case studies, role-playing and simulations, as these methods relate to their experiences. These methods keep participants involved with the lesson. Dewey in the 1930's suggested that the role of the teacher is to guide and facilitate learning based on life experiences rather than on expert or formal authority and use the information to make a connection between what is known and what we are trying to teach. Teachers can incorporate adult experiences in their lessons and can emphasize learning together to get everyone involved. As a result, all may benefit from the instruction.

Knowles (1980), a respected leader in adult education, explained that the learning climate, both physical and psychological, should be carefully constructed for acceptance, respect, and support. As explained in chapter four, teachers need to prepare the environment where learning takes place, considering proper light, sound, seating arrangement, and temperature. Knowles acknowledged that such preparation encourages a desire to learn and motivates the learners as they get involved with the process. Affective and intellectual characteristics influence learning. The affective domain includes learners' morals, beliefs, values, and attitudes. Intellectual characteristics include reading ability and the processing of information. The following section focuses on some other adult characteristics.

Adult Learners Have Certain Characteristics

Knowles and other adult educators recognized these adult characteristics for instance:

- Adults have multiple roles: parent, breadwinner, leader in the home.
- They have more life experiences than children (they have had varied experiences and may be going through transitions in life, from school to work, or to marriage, or through a divorce)
- They are task oriented (want to apply knowledge immediately.)
- Because of these characteristics, teachers must meet adults' specific needs.

They must understand:
- Why adults enroll in a particular class
- What they are hoping to learn
- How to provide support and encouragement
- How to gather background information

Because of adult learning styles, teachers must:

- Ensure the climate is non-threatening
- Relate learning to previous knowledge as a bridge to new learning

In planning for adult instruction, teachers need to know their audiences. In addition:

- Teachers need to adjust to the life stages of aging adults
- They must consider decline in vision, delays in reaction time, and,
- Understand that short-term memory is limited.

Because we are different, we learn differently. One aspect of a teacher's job is facilitating learning through understanding different learning styles.

Learning Styles

Just as each individual is different, so is his or her learning style. There are several measures of learning styles available, and some measures are very similar because they require individuals to fit themselves into categories or models that sometimes overlap. These learning models are on a continuum; each person could place himself or herself somewhere on the continuum on one or more of these models or scales or poles.

Carl Jung (1923) said people are different in fundamental ways even though they have the same multitude of instincts to drive them from within. He tabulated different psychological types from which the Myers Briggs Psychological Type inventory emerged. This inventory proposes there are many psychological types. It labels some people as introverts or extroverts, sensors or intuitors, thinkers or feelers, judgers or perceivers. Different psychological types have different learning preferences.

A simpler model proposes that people are either perceptual or structural learners. The next section provides information on some learning style models, beginning with a discussion of the perceptual and structural learners.

Perceptual vs. Structural Learners

Perceptual learners may be visual, verbal, and kinaesthetic. Structural learners are sequential, hierarchal, and global. Do you feel you fit into any of these categories? Hill (1976) breaks these down further. Think about them as you determine to what extent you may fit into any of the following categories. Check for any overlap as you think about these categories:

- Auditory – finding meaning through listening, specifically the spoken word.
- Visual – finding meaning through reading or symbols
- Olfactory – finding meaning in smelling or scents
- Savoury – find meaning in taste
- Tactile – meaning through touch
- Emphatic – meaning through feelings
- Kinaesthetic – meaning through non-verbal means
- Esthetical – meaning through beauty (picture the garden of Eden)

You may fall into many of these categories but not to the same extent on any one. That is, you may be not only visual, but also need audio methods and even a bit of hands-on learning, which is kinaesthetic. It is important to realize that people do learn differently, and each has preferences; some people probably even change their preferences depending on what they are learning. If someone is learning a new recipe, which category or categories would be more important? Of course, some will enjoy tasting to evaluate the level of perfection of the food; most would want hands-on experience as well. If you were teaching someone to assemble a bicycle, which category would you recommend? Hands-on experience would be appropriate. Some would want to concentrate on the big picture, the finished product, while others may focus on the parts that make up the whole bicycle. How would you teach the kinaesthetic learner? Reading and listening alone is not enough for this type; they need to *do* something in order to learn.

If you are teaching about the whole armour of God (Ephesians 6:13-19), the auditory learners would quickly understand and even have a mental picture; the visual learners may want symbols or pictures of the armour.

On the other hand, if you were learning a process, like building a model, what method would you use? You have to build the base first and follow a procedure. Sequencing would be very important. A step-by-step approach would be important in understanding how things fit together. It might also be helpful to show the finished product so the students can see the desired end result.

There are other ways of categorizing learners. Another simple model of categorization of learners is as dependent, independent or collaborative.

Dependent, Independent, and Collaborative

> Glen Johnson notes some students are "dependent prone" and need highly structured settings in which to function, whereas others are "independent prone" and require greater flexibility and freedom. Barbara Schneider Fuhrman and Ronne Jacobs added to this dichotomy a third category, the "collaborative style", and developed a model that discriminates three classroom learning styles, the dependent style, the collaborate style and the independent style. (Fuhrman and Grasha p. 114)

Dependent learners may be passive, waiting on the teacher to provide information and later reflecting on this information. Supplemented with teachers' notes, lecture would be fine. Independent learners may prefer to read on their own, make their own notes, and interpret information without much help from the teacher. Independent learners come to their own specific conclusion on any material they read.

Educators perceive people with collaborative learning styles as co-learners. Teachers and students make knowledge together, as in working on projects, instead of the teacher being the provider of knowledge and the student being the recipient of knowledge. Bosworth and Hamilton, in their article "Knowledge as Co-conspirator: Knowledge as Authority in Collaborative Learning" (1994), argued that students still need an authoritative presence, and the transition of knowledge must become part of the experience of the participant. Active learning is important for such a transition to take place.

Another model that involves experience is the Kolb model. Kolb bases his experiential model on learning that is sometimes called action learning, reflection in action, and praxis.

Kolb's Experiential Model

Kolb says his model combines experience, perception, cognition and behaviour, unlike rationalist and behavioural learning, which focuses on recall, memorization, and learning by rote. Kolb's model describes learning as a cycle that begins with the student's personal involvement in specific experiences. According to Kolb, the learner's experience is important for reflection, and he or she can present many viewpoints to find meaning of the learning material. The learner will draw his or her own conclusion from theory. Kolb's uses a quadrant to illustrate his model. You can make a quadrant by drawing two lines that intersect to make a cross or a tilted "X". On the vertical line, students will move from concrete experience at the top end to abstract at the bottom end. On the horizontal line, students will move from active experiments on the left to reflections on the extreme right. Each section represents a quadrant. Into each quadrant, Kolb fits four levels of learning and four types of learners.

Kolb labels these types as accommodators if they fall into the top right of the quadrant; as assimilators if they fall into the bottom right side; as convergers if their fall into the top left section; and as divergers if they fall into the bottom left side (Kolb's Learning Styles). Following from the top right to bottom right, then from bottom left to top left creates a cycle, which Kolb calls a learning cycle. Students begin with concrete experiences and their personal involvement with information, such as examples and pictures (feelers). They may move to reflective observation by learning principles or concepts and reflecting on them, trying to understand their meaning, by journaling, discussion and brainstorming (watchers). Abstract conceptualization will interest those who can use learning to draw logical conclusions from analogies (thinkers). Active experimentation refers to students' use of content and their interaction with it (doers). They then add their own conclusions, possibly through using case studies, to discover and evaluate new experiences and make recommendations. By using Kolb's model, people can identify their stage of learning as feelers, watchers, thinkers or doers when involved in experiential learning.

This type of learning experience is also known as experiential learning. It relates very well to Transformative Learning, which is learning that produces change in a person's way of thinking or acting. The transformative learning experience causes reflection, which drives the learner to make changes based on new perspectives.

Transformative Learning

Transformative learning is experiential learning that produces life change. This means that the learning changes a person's ways of thinking in such a way that they think differently after the learning experience. Outsiders can recognize this change. This change may occur because of personal development, change in action, attitude, and reflection. Jack Mezirow (1990), an adult education expert, said, "Transformative learning is aimed at helping the individual to become more aware and critical of assumptions in order to actively engage in changing those that are not adaptive or are inadequate for problem-solving" (p.159). He believes that adulthood is a time for reassessing assumptions people learnt earlier in life to see if they still make sense, and to challenge the validity of these assumptions.

The learner must be able to reason and not just accept social realities defined by others. It is the reasoning and reassessing of values that causes a transformation to take place. Such a transformation takes place when someone comes to know the Lord. When people listen to testimonies, they are amazed at the life-changing stories and the impact this new information has had on people's lives. A person's experience of having lived through a traumatic event to tell their story is significant enough to cause a life-changing experience. Romeo Dallaire, the UN commander who witnessed genocide in Rwanda, said publicly that the experience changed his way of thinking and his life.

Another illustration would be the story of Saul of Tarsus in the book of Acts, chapter nine. Saul was on his way to Damascus to persecute the Jewish Christians. As he traveled, suddenly there was a bright light from heaven. It stunned him and he could not see. What could be a more disorienting dilemma? He had to stop and reflect on this experience. God planned it so that Saul had to meet with Christians who, through the Holy Spirit, caused him to see again, and instructed him in the way of Christianity. During his dark days of blindness, Saul did some serious thinking about how he had been persecuting the Christians, who were now the very ones helping him. He acted on these new experiences and revelations. During this time, more reflection and evaluation of his old ways would lead him to a change of values and attitude. The result was a transformation in thinking and a definite desire to worship the true God and not persecute the Christians. He even changed his name to Paul to show that he had a new personality and beliefs that made him want to share and lead others to Christ. He followed in obedience by getting baptized, praying, and preaching.

One can use the experiences in others' lives to encourage transformative learning in one's own everyday life. A father loved to tell stories to make a point aimed at changing attitudes and values. He recalled a time when his older boys were annoying a younger sibling. He then told a story of what happened to him when he did the same in his boyhood days. The father shared with his children how as a child he used to tease a younger boy by calling him derogatory names. He did that for a couple of years, but one day, he had to stop. In adolescence, the younger boy grew faster than he did and decided he would take the teasing no more. He therefore planned a strategy he was sure would stop the teasing. He waited for the teasing, then picked up the offender and threw him to the ground. The father told how his head spun and how he had lain there lifeless, trying to figure out what had gone wrong. That was enough, and the father never teased the younger boy again. This story illustrated a disorienting experience, an observation stage, thinking and planning, and then action to change original perception. This type of learning involves making informed choices on how to act on new perspectives. The learner must have the will to act on his or her new convictions based on critical reflection and consciousness rising to affect change.

Mezirow (1990) states, "Every adult educator has a central responsibility for fostering critical reflection and transformative learning" (p.1). This reflection is what teachers want to encourage in their classes, to present information that would raise consciousness and stimulate people to reflect on new perspectives. Dart & Boulton-Lewis in *Teaching and Learning in Higher Education* spoke of the holist using information for personal benefit and going beyond the information given. They refer to a deep approach that helps the learner to understand and make meaning of it instead of simple memorization. Helping class participants to think beyond the obvious message, and seek implications of the lesson, will encourage deeper learning.

John Dewey in 1933 suggested that the role of the teacher is to guide and facilitate learning based on life experiences rather than on expert or formal authority. Teachers can emphasize learning together, getting everyone involved, as learning together will be of benefit to the entire class.

Learning Activities

The first day of class is particularly important since it sets the stage for what is to follow. Cranton stated, "most people begin by determining the learners' educational level, age or age range, prior knowledge of the subject, previous experiences and mother tongue" (1997, in *Planning Instruction for Adult Learners*, p. 15). This information helps in planning activities for the rest of the course, and the level of instruction, from basic knowledge, comprehension, application, synthesis and evaluation (from Bloom's taxonomy of knowledge levels). Learning activities may be geared towards student groups and personalities. Teachers will plan activities to accommodate most of the participants in the class. Some students will want hands-on activities while others will appreciate discussion or role-playing to facilitate learning. Activities will depend on the topic or goal of the lesson. A discussion on goal setting and learning objectives follows.

Learning Objectives

It is important that adults know at the beginning of the class what they are expected to learn. Teachers enlighten students by using learning objectives. These objectives explain what the learner will do or learn by the by the end of the lesson or class. The teacher could set one or more objectives. At the end of the session, the student participant will know something, understand something, or be able to do or distinguish something. One has to write learning objectives in such a way that the teacher or leader will be able to measure some accomplishment. For example, the objective could state that at the end of the session, the participants will be able to list the fruit of the spirit, explain the evangelical meaning of baptism, or be able to compare two versions of a story.

At another level, the learner will be able to comprehend concepts or apply principles to solve problems. The teacher may want to assess change in values or attitudes. Values and attitudes are integral parts of Christian teaching. The objective may be to acquire a particular skill; for example, to be able to counsel and nurture new Christians. The student may need to be able to evaluate topics or books to see if they meet certain criteria.

Most adult learners will want to know the lesson plan, the sequencing of activities and the duration of the lesson so that they may be able to anticipate when the lesson is coming to end. Proper planning and giving information ahead of time reduces anxiety. Once the teacher plans objectives, the teacher or leader must consider and decide on the delivery method or methods that will best meet the objective.

Delivery Methods

Because people learn differently, using several delivery methods will enhance learning and ensure that at any given time there will be some participants learning. Knowles (1980) and others recommend some teaching methods that can be utilized in class. As stated earlier, adults like questioning, discussion, problem solving, group work, case studies, role-playing and simulations. These methods relate to adults' learning experience, that is, how teachers keep adult students involved with the lesson.

Questioning at different levels encourages critical thinking and learning. Bloom (1956) recommends that questioning should be at these different levels: knowledge, comprehension, application, analysis and synthesis. Using these levels will challenge the student to think critically and examine different perspectives. At the knowledge level, the question may ask for a list of the prophets. At the comprehension level, the teacher may ask for examples of prophets, groups of similar prophets, or attributes of Christian values. Students may be able to act as a prophet, or distinguish prophets from non-prophets, or even prepare a profile of a prophet and state the significant teaching or message of that prophet.

There are different forms of questioning. For instance, reflective questions determine if there has been a change in values and attitudes of the student. In Lee and Barnet's *Using Reflective Questioning to Promote Collaborative Dialogue* (1994), they describe reflective questioning as a technique in which someone prepares and asks questions designed to encourage respondents to use their knowledge in such a manner that skills, experiences, attitudes, beliefs, and values become transparent. They support reflective questioning because it appropriately demands thoughtful self-examination. This type of questioning lends itself very well to discovering how and if students are responding to Christian values and attitudes. They recommend clarifying questions that call on respondents' experiences.

Not all material is conducive to questioning; sometimes discussion will better bring the subject to life and facilitate learning the points of reference about a certain topic. In discussions, teachers need to make sure there is balance between talkers and listeners and that most participants are involved. This method, carefully managed, will keep the class involved and the teacher in control. The leader could begin with a broad theme and welcome different interpretations. Inviting another person's perspective may also serve to enlighten others.

Relational topics may be addressed better using role-play. Role reversal helps some participants to think analytically and understand others' perspectives. Another way of doing this is to use simulation of different situations. Simulation helps to avoid the possible judgment of personal situations.

Simulations will help participants with decision-making and understanding the consequences of their decisions. The case method is a type of simulation of a real life situation. Teachers use this method successfully in adult education since participants have life experiences that can help in evaluating the situation presented in the specific case, and in decision-making. Using case methods can bring to life an otherwise dull topic.

Though prevalent in post-secondary education, the lecture method may not always be preferable for teaching adults in a Bible study. If the lecture method is used, it can be enhanced with stories, allegories, demonstrations, and real-life examples, as well as by utilizing audience participation in some way. Some teachers find the lecture method boring unless they make an effort to add humour to keep it interesting. If teachers are using this common method, Griffin (1993) suggests using supplements like visuals and illustrations. By using humour and addressing problems that interest students, the teacher could offer solutions to their problems. Regardless of the delivery method, an order of presentation is necessary.

Presentation

After developing learning objectives and choosing delivery methods, be sure that participants are aware of these early in the presentation. A systematic approach may be helpful. At the start of each lesson, the participants must know the learning expectations, so in order to sequence instruction, use a systematic approach. Some people like to use the logical sequential method, reasoning from the known to the unknown, whereas others prefer to go from the unknown to the known. (For instance, in assembling a bike, you can show the finished product or you may begin with identifying the parts.) Anticipate the type of questions the audience is likely to ask, and be prepared to answer those questions. In any case, follow these steps:

- Tell the objective of the lesson. Explain its purpose. Consider participants' interest.
- Present the details, verbally, in print or using audio video equipment.

- Discuss the story. Look for truths and consequences, advantages and disadvantages, grace and love as applicable.
- Seek implications of the story from participants. Show or ask participants how they think the story may be applicable to their lives.
- End the lesson with a summary of the main points.
- Consider the amount of time you have for the presentation, and schedule your timing to allow for all the actions already listed.

McClanahan and McClanahan (2002) recommend a variety of teaching strategies and interaction with students to promote understanding, and to help students appreciate the value of a lesson and its application. A subject like biology would definitely need this kind of interaction. It could also help if teachers use props for illustration.

In addition, teachers may want to use technological equipment and computer software to assist in presentations. Not every classroom may be equipped for computer technology. Overheads may be just as effective. Regardless of the stage of technology, use the equipment effectively.

Using Technology

The use of technological equipment and computer software is now prevalent in teaching. Preparation for these presentations may save time and allow information to flow smoothly. The disadvantage is that teachers may need more preparation time, and software and equipment may be costly. Visual aides such as pictures and outlines can be very helpful. When power point slides and overheads are used, remember to use a large font. Do not clutter slides with too much information. Show one thought or principle at a time so that students may concentrate fully on one idea or subject. Also leave a slide on long enough to allow participants to read it and possibly take notes if they choose to. Teachers may judge timing by reading the slide silently as participants read them aloud. Students want to follow the presentation and not feel they missed something. Students can judge how teachers do on presentations when they evaluate its effectiveness. Teachers too need feedback on how well students are learning.

Student Evaluation

At the end of a lesson, the teacher needs to know to what extent he or she accomplished his or her objectives. This evaluation can be formative or summative, depending on the circumstances. For a formative evaluation, teachers can use simple generic questionnaires at the end of each lesson. The answer to these questions could expose teachers to students' concerns and assist them in improving their presentations to suit the participants' needs. The teacher may want the student to make a list of names or topics studied.

As a summative evaluation, the teacher may want the student to provide examples to prove he or she understood the lesson. The teacher may want to ask a student to volunteer to summarize the lesson or demonstrate their learning in some way. Normally in an academic setting, teachers use formative and summative evaluation methods. Adult educators advise that formal evaluation using testing is not a good idea for adults in this setting, as this method may appear to be threatening and cause participants some anxiety that may lead to avoiding classes. In a Sunday school setting, formative evaluations may be effective if teachers use a "fill in the blanks" type of form which participants may work on in class alone or together, or alone at home later.

One cannot assume that this simple evaluation form accurately reflects what the students learned from the lesson, however, because the benefits of the lesson can occur long after the class is over. This summary may only show how much the student understood or is willing to share at one point. Therefore, teachers also may want to use another method of evaluation.

Kramp and Humphreys (1990-1991) shared their research on using narrative and self-assessment. They proposed self-assessment as an activity in which students would incorporate past learning into their present learning and evaluate themselves based on how they saw their learning as making choices and decisions. They recommended in *Narrative, Self-assessment and the Reflective Learner* that self-assessment helps students to make judgments and change what they deem appropriate. Their research found that this type of learning allows students to gain insights and set directions for the future. It also allows teachers time for reflection on their role and individual students' needs. This type of evaluation may work well for those teaching the Christian faith. Teachers who want to find out how they are doing will find teacher evaluation tools very useful.

Teacher Evaluation

Most teachers want to know how they are doing, and most appreciate some form of feedback. After a particular session or course, student feedback on instruction will draw the teacher's attention to their overall performance and presentation skills. This type of evaluation will help teachers to correct unforeseen errors and prepare for the next round of classes. Ongoing evaluation may be better to help a teacher to correct problems before the end of the session. Either the teacher or the student may do this. Teachers' intuition can help them sound out student's responses through questioning or even through the look of confusion or contentment on the participants' faces. Teachers must look for cues. You can pick up these cues by observing students' behaviour. Through prayer and the leading of the Holy Spirit, teachers can perceive the situation and provide encouragement for students as needed.

Another important part of teaching is content, the subject of the lesson. Although this handbook is limited to exclude a major discussion on content, some reference to curriculum or topics included in a lesson or a course needs discussion. The next section provides some insight into content.

Content

In a Bible study, the Bible is usually the main source of reference. Timothy said that the Word of God is the source of all truth and should be taught and learnt.

> All scripture is inspired by God and profitable for teaching, for reproof, for correction, for training in righteousness; so that the man of God may be adequate, equipped for every good work. (2 Timothy 3:16-17)

Although content is not the focus of this handbook, one cannot ignore saying something about content in a chapter on intellectual preparation. It is good to emphasize again that the Bible is the main source of content for teaching the Christian faith. In Paul's epistle to the Philippians, he prayed:

> That your love may abound still more and more in real knowledge and all discernment, so that you may approve the things that are excellent, in order to be sincere and blameless until the day of Christ; having been filled with the fruit of righteousness which comes through Jesus Christ, to the glory and praise of God. (Philippians 1:9-11)

Even though we use the Bible as the main source of teaching, there are reputable writers on the Christian faith that leaders and teachers can consult. Teaching resources permeate Christian literature. Billy Graham is a good example of a person who writes for Christians. Other recognizable authors are Dr. Dobson from Focus on the Family, Charles Colson, Charles Stanley, Dr. Neil Anderson, Garry Smalley and Beth Moore, to name a few. These writers provide valuable perspectives on the faith and are very credible, not only in the Christian world, but in the secular world as well. People rely on these writers because of their life experiences and their wisdom.

Solomon says, "The beginning of wisdom is: acquire wisdom" (Proverbs 4:7). God's people must truly present His Word clearly and truthfully. Participants may relate to spiritually seeking people who write about God. These writings are valuable resources for teachers of the Christian faith. However, knowing what your Bible has to say is essential for teaching the Christian faith, and credible resources should serve to assist teachers.

Some scripture references in the next section will reinforce what the Bible says about content.

SCRIPTURE REFERENCES

Throughout the scriptures, many passages encourage teachers. God has never left His people without instruction and the leading of the Holy Spirit. The assurance of the leading of the Holy Spirit is a booster for teachers' confidence.

David provided this reassurance in the Psalms.

> I will instruct you and teach you in the way which you should go. I will counsel you with My eye upon you. (Psalm 32:8)

God allowed Daniel to be taught, and he used his knowledge for God's work (Daniel 9:22) God gave Daniel instruction, insight, and truth with understanding. Education has always been valued. Nebuchadnezzar, king of Babylon, ordered learned men to teach the Israelites. He ordered them to teach them the literature and language of the Chaldeans. They had to be educated for three years (v. 54) to enter the king's personal service. The stipulation of who should teach includes those showing intelligence in every branch of wisdom, endowed with understanding and discerning knowledge, and who had ability for serving in the king's court.

David speaking to Solomon said:

> Now behold, there are the divisions of the priests and the Levites for all the service of the house of God, and every willing man of any skill will be with you in all the work for all kinds of service. (1 Chronicles 28:21)

In the epistle to the Ephesians, Paul prayed, "That the God of our Lord Jesus Christ, the Father of glory, may give to you a spirit of wisdom and of revelation in the knowledge of Him" (Ephesians 1:17).

The foregoing scriptures deal with knowledge of spiritual

things. Teachers of the Christian faith need to be conversant with God's Word and understand His plans for the human race. We will now turn our attention to some specific intellectual preparation steps that will enhance teaching.

INTELLECTUAL PREPARATION STEPS

Buskist and William (2000) prepared some steps for teaching assistants at the university level. These steps are also important in adult education, and teachers may use them when teaching adult audiences. These steps are summarized and explained below:

1. **Use a warm up exercise**. This may be a recent discussion of events in the newspapers relating to the subject matter, or a joke. This is also known as an icebreaker because it relaxes the audience.
2. **Create a strong presence**. The implication is that the audience will recognize the person in authority before that person even makes a statement.
3. **Link similar topics to show connection**. The transition statements show connection of one topic to another. You can relate new learning to a topic already known by asking questions to show the link to the lesson.
4. **Make an outline of material to help with organization**. This allows the participants to follow the presentation and know what comes next.
5. **Make eye contact**. Eye contact is important and can help the facilitator to read whether the participants understand the topic, have doubts about it, and of course, if they are paying attention or daydreaming.
6. **Ask simple questions**. Simple questions only need easy answers, and this encourages the participants to speak freely and confidently.
7. **Acknowledge interaction with students** even if the answers are

incorrect. In this case, the facilitator may ask for another perspective on the topic.

8. **Repeat a question or rephrase it** so all will hear and understand it. By doing this, the facilitator is giving the participants more time to understand the question and think about an answer.

9. **Anticipate the type of questions** the audience is likely to ask, and be prepared to answer.

The exercises below will reinforce the steps listed above and help with their application.

INTELLECTUAL EXERCISE

1. How do you plan to assess the learning styles of your students and address them? _____
   _____
   _____
   _____
   _____
   _____

2. Write a learning objective for your first lesson. _____
   _____
   _____
   _____
   _____
   _____
   _____

3. Prepare an outline for your presentation. _____
   _____
   _____
   _____
   _____

Preparing to Teach God's Word

4. What learning activities do you feel would help you and your students enjoy learning the lesson? _____
_____
_____
_____
_____
_____
_____

5. Prepare a lesson summary for the end of your first class. _____
_____
_____
_____
_____
_____

6. Write a question that would solicit an answer that would tell you your students have understood the lesson. _____
_____
_____
_____
_____
_____

7. Write a reflective question that would clarify any doubts about student's understanding of the topic presented. _____
_____
_____
_____
_____
_____

8. How do you plan to evaluate your students' understanding of the lesson? _____

9. How do you plan to evaluate your teaching, to see how well you are doing? _____

10. What type of warm up exercise do you feel is appropriate for your class? _____

11. How would you respond to participants' incorrect answers without making the person feel embarrassed? _____

CHAPTER SUMMARY

Intellectual preparation focuses on being ready to teach the subject or course content, and adapting teaching and learning principles to accommodate adult audiences. This chapter described adult education skills and techniques, including selecting teaching methods, learning activities, understanding learning styles, setting learning objectives, and choosing evaluation methods. These tasks are essential components of intellectual preparation. These preparation steps are important aids for students' and teachers' success. These steps explain that you can choose learning activities to motivate adults and encourage learning at several levels. Discussion, problem solving, group work, case studies, and role-play, all keep adults interested and engaged with the subject. Learning objectives that you present at the beginning of the class will prepare student participants for the lesson and reduce anxiety. They create expectations of what students will learn in the session. The course or session outline informs students of the stages of presentation. If students know ahead of time what to expect, they may anticipate the learning and have some input into the teaching. They may feel positive about the class and be more willing to participate.

The discussion on spiritual, emotional, physical and intellectual considerations provides a model for teachers to follow as they prepare to teach the Word of God. This chapter on intellectual preparation may be a priority for those people with no teaching experience. The next chapter summarizes the handbook and places teachers and teaching in a biblical context.

CHAPTER 6

Summary and Conclusion

All scripture is inspired by God and profitable for teaching, for reproof, for correction, for training in righteousness; so that the man of God may be adequate, equipped for every good work (2 Timothy 3:16-17).

This chapter summarizes the information presented in this handbook, including:

    God's Gifts and Promises
    Purpose Revisited
    Lesson In a Nutshell
    Dependence on God
    Scripture Reference
    The End of the Journey
    Concluding Comments
    Handbook Evaluation Questions

GOD'S GIFTS AND PROMISES

This handbook began on the premise that all people are sinners and no one is deserving of God's grace and glory, but God offers salvation. Salvation is a gift. Along with salvation, God acknowledged that people might have several practical spiritual gifts or callings. Some are prophets, some evangelists, some pastors, and some teachers; all are to be engaged in the service of our Lord and Saviour, Jesus Christ (Ephesians 4:12-13). It is from this premise that Christians believe they should strive for holiness and obedience to God's Word. The Lord wants His people to reach greater heights, and these heights may be achieved through obedience and studying His Word. As teachers and others study God's Word, they are in a constant state of change, a metamorphosis that can transform them into what God wants them to be. Lifelong learning facilitates this change and is important to all Christians as they continue to mature in their faith. In the maturing process, one can take a leading role by guiding others. Preparation for guiding others is explicit in this handbook. To equip people, a holistic approach using the proverbial guitar and its strings illustrates how teachers may further prepare themselves to reach others for Christ. Teachers and leaders of the Christian faith may benefit from paying attention to the strings of the proverbial guitar presented in the pervious chapters.

PURPOSE REVISITED

The purpose of the handbook was to introduce some teaching techniques and make some recommendations on teaching preparation that will enhance reaching people for Christ. It emphasized the proverbial guitar and strings introduced by Cranton (1993). The strings of this proverbial guitar illustrate how a holistic approach to teaching brings meaning to those spreading the "good news" of the Christian faith. The strings emphasized in this handbook are spiritual, emotional, intuitive and relational, physical, and intellectual considerations. For the purpose of this handbook, there is a combination of emotional and intuitional strings and a full discussion of the spiritual, physical, and intellectual strings. The handbook covered many ways to help teachers improve, develop, and equip themselves for service. Its focus was Christian teachings from the Holy Bible. Appendix 1 provides a sample lesson that may help those who want to pursue a biblical teaching career in Christian education. To summarize the text, a miniature lesson follows. The theme is, "Do to others as you would have them do to you" (Luke 6:31, NIV).

LESSON IN A NUTSHELL

When preparing for a lesson, a teacher may like to consider using an "ice breaker" to get students' attention. If this is the first lesson of a series of lessons, then introductions of teacher and participants should precede introduction of the topic. Before beginning the lesson, the teacher should try to ensure that students are comfortable, that they know something about each other, and the reason for attending the class. One way to do this would be to have students introduce themselves and simply tell the class in a sentence or two their learning expectations. Alternatively, a teacher could allow any two students to become familiar with each other first by engaging in an enquiring conversation. After making this initial social contact, each of the two students may introduce the other to the class. In addition, teachers may prepare a simple form students can complete to gain personal information that students may be too shy to disclose to the class but may want to share with the teacher. The teacher may also have specific questions concerning the students' background and interests.

Once introductions are over, the teacher may want to provide an outline of the session and perhaps start with a story. A relevant story may arouse curiosity and get students to focus. Here is one illustration a father used to teach his children.

Tommy always took his toys apart to see how they were made. Tommy went to sleep. The next thing he knew, a giant had laid a heavy hand on Tommy. "Ouch!" Tommy yelled, which startled the giant, making him pull his hand away quickly. Tommy heard the giant then reply, "I wonder how he works?"

This story may instigate some discussion questions such as who did what to whom and why? Were there consequences for the action, and what was the reaction? You see, Tommy used to dismember his toys. So in his dreams, he learned that he too, could be dismembered, thereby reaping what he sowed.

After this discussion, students may be ready for content. Presentation would follow the introduction of the lesson. Remember, the subject is about doing good things for others. A teacher may want to introduce the main point at this time, including scripture references. In the Kings James version of the Bible, Luke 6:31 states, "As ye would that men should do to you, do ye also to them likewise." The translation of the New American Standard version of Luke 6:31 states, "Treat others the same way you want them to treat you." The point of the lesson when illustrated should stimulate discussion questions.

As discussion questions follow, allow participants to reflect on the points of the lesson, think of truth and consequences, and what application the lesson may have in their lives. Students may want to share experiences of how this lesson applied early in their lives or how it helped them in certain situations. Sharing may help to stimulate thought processes towards application of the principle to those who do not already apply it to situations in their lives. They may be some people in the discussion group who may reflect on the hurt and pain they inflict on others. On the other hand, God does not want a tit-for-tat world. Forgiveness is the antidote.

One could summarize the lesson with another illustration. It could be similar to a seed of love planted in the heart of a person. This person should expect growth as he or she reflects on the principle of loving one another and doing unto others even better than people do for him or her. Participants need to value the next step, which is to do something nice for others. Realize that this maturing love of people will reflect the degree of dependence on our Lord and Saviour Jesus Christ and our obedience to His Word.

DEPENDING ON HIM

Paul the apostle used his second epistle to Timothy to tell people that scripture should be the main source for teaching and keeping Christian people on the Christian path. Other scriptures reinforce this principle. The following quotations point out significant Christian doctrines and values. God has called people to do His will (Philippians 1:6). Christians must strive to do good "so that you will prove yourselves to be blameless and innocent, children of God above reproach in the midst of a crooked and perverse generation, among whom you appear as lights in the world" (Philippians 2:15). Continuing and maturing in the faith requires discipline. Again, the apostle Paul was sure to explain how Christians may continue to mature in Christ.

SCRIPTURE REFERENCES

> Therefore, take up the full armor of God, so that you will be able to resist in the evil day, and having done everything, to stand firm (Ephesians 6:13.).

Paul uses the army uniform as a metaphor to illustrate how Christians should dress. He continued:

> Stand firm therefore, having girded your loins with truth, and having put on the breastplate of righteousness, and having Shod your feet with the preparation of the gospel of peace; in addition to all, taking up the shield of faith with which you will be able to extinguish all the flaming arrows of the evil one. And take the helmet of salvation, and the sword of the spirit, which is the word of God (Ephesians 6:14-17).

Jesus urged that people should use their talents wisely. The path may not always be smooth. Sometimes things will get rough, but Christians will survive by the grace of God and his Holy Spirit.

God never leaves His people comfortless. Teachers and others can claim this promise. David said:

> He will give his angels charge concerning you; to guard you in all your ways. They will bear you up in their hands, that you do not strike your foot against a stone. (Psalm 91:11-12)

These comforting words are still applicable in these days. Memorizing this verse and reflecting on it could bring comfort in tough times. Teaching is a stressful endeavour, and teachers need encouragement. Moses said this when he knew he would not enter the Promised Land:

> Be strong and courageous, do not be afraid or tremble at them, for the Lord your God is the one who goes with you. He will not fail you or forsake you. (Deuteronomy 31:6)

During tough times the Lord will go with you also. He will keep you under His wings, says the Psalmist. As we strive for holiness and examine ourselves to prepare to teach and lead others to Jesus, let us remember: Christians must embrace holiness and examine themselves as they prepare to teach and lead others to Jesus. No mountain should be too high or valley too low if God is with you.

No temptation is too great.

> No temptation has overtaken you but such as is common to man; and God is faithful, who will not allow you to be tempted beyond what you are able, but with the temptation will provide the way of escape also, so that you will be able to endure it. (1 Corinthians 10:13)

THE END OF THE JOURNEY

There will come a time in every teacher's life when retirement is inevitable. At that time, it would be great if a teacher feels fulfilled from a satisfying teaching career. It would be exciting if one feels confident that he or she has done his or her best for the Lord. The end of the journey is predictable. Elvis Presley sang, "When you come to the end of your journey, He'll understand and say well done."

In the parable of the talents, the master delighted in the one who used his talent wisely and efficiently, and rewarded him. The master said:

> Well done, good and faithful slave. You were faithful with a few things, I will put you in charge of many things; enter into the joy of your master (Matthew 25:21)

This statement is similar to what Paul the apostle said when he came to the end of his journey. He was satisfied that he did all that he could to propagate the gospel of God. He ran and he finished his race.

This walk with God is a daily journey. It takes time, effort, and continual self-evaluation to know if one is doing the right thing. As David said:

> Search me, oh God, and know my heart; Try me and know my anxious thoughts; and see if there be any

hurtful way in me, and lead me in the everlasting way (Psalm 139 23-24)

When Solomon had completed building the house of the Lord, he had a vision. In the vision he heard this: "If my people who are called by My name humble themselves and pray and seek My face and turn from their wicked ways, then I will hear from heaven, will forgive their sin and will heal their land." (2 Chronicles 7:14)

Teachers and leaders must consider these words seriously. A preacher once said that God gave people a conscience to help them examine themselves. A good conscience will act as a thermometer. The temperature will rise when people are not complying with God's laws, indicating that there is a problem in their lives. God is good. In fact, He is excellent in every way and His promises are fantastic. He will sustain His people!

CHAPTER SUMMARY

This teaching handbook was prepared for those aspiring to teach adults and reach them for Christ, whether in teaching Sunday school or through leading a Bible study. The handbook demonstrates a holistic approach to teaching and learning. It is by no means all inclusive of the steps teachers must take to enhance learning and to prepare themselves for teaching. Teachers will have to couple their knowledge of teaching with their experiences in the classroom to ensure that they come up with the right combination of techniques for a specific class or group. Each group of students is different.

The important thing is to be prepared spiritually, emotionally, physically, and intellectually for teaching God's Word and making a difference in people's lives.

In conclusion:

> Though you have not seen Him, you love Him, and though you do not see Him now, but believe in Him, you greatly rejoice with joy inexpressible and full of glory. (1 Peter 1:8)

CLOSING EXERCISE

1. What sections of this manual did you find useful? _____
   _____
   _____
   _____
   _____
   _____

2. Which part of the manual do you feel needed more information or explanation? _____
   _____
   _____
   _____
   _____
   _____

3. Would you like to offer suggestions for improving this manual?
   _____
   _____
   _____
   _____
   _____
   _____

4. What suggestions about teaching adults did you implement in your classes? _____
   _____
   _____
   _____
   _____

CONCLUSION

This handbook was prepared to assist people preparing to teach Sunday school, lead a Bible study or reach others for Christ. It addresses topics that will enhance teaching and also provides advice on dealing with adult learners. It provides several suggestions for planning and organizing classrooms, course material, and facilitating learning. The handbook began with the premise that, although all people are sinners, they are not alone. God sent His Holy Spirit to walk alongside His people. God has expectations of His people. He gave them many gifts to use for His glory. You may enhance your gift for teaching by preparing spiritually, emotionally, physically and intellectually. God encourages His people in many ways through the scriptures. There are rewards for those who are obedient to His Word, accepting the challenge to go into the entire world and spread the gospel. Walk in such a way that when you come to the end of your journey, the Lord will be pleased and ready to say "Well done, good and faithful slave; you were faithful with a few things, I will put you in charge of many things; enter into the joy of your master." (Matthew 25: 21)

Please send comments to parker77@telus.net.

References

Barber-Stein, Thelma & Kompg. Michael. *Craft of Teaching Adults.* 3rd Ed. Toronto: Irwin Publishers, 2001.

Bloom, B. S., Krathwohl, D. R. Taxonomy of Educational Objectives: The classification of Educational Goals, by a committee of college and university examiners. Handbook 1. Cognitive Domain. New York: Longmans, Green, 1956.

Buskist, William. *The Teaching Professor.* Feb 2002, Vol. 16, No. 2. Madison: Magna Publications Inc., 2002.

Clark, Carlolinn, "Learning Environment for Women's Adult Development: Bridges Towards Change." In *New Directions for Adult and Continuing Education #65.* San Francisco: Jossey-Bass.

Cranton, Patricia, & Western, Cynthia, B. "Considering the Audience." In *Planning Instruction for Adult Learners.* Toronto: Wall and Thompson, 1989.

Cranton, Patricia. *Planning Instruction for Adults.* Toronto: Wall and Thompson, 1989.

Cranton, Patricia. "Principles of Adult Learning." In *Planning Instruction for Adult Learners.* Toronto: Wall and Thompson, 1989.

Cranton, Patricia *Working with Adult Learners.* Toronto: Wall and Thompson, 1989.

Dart H. and Boulton-Lewis G. "Approaches to Learning and Forms of Understanding." In *Teaching and Learning in Higher Education.* Sydney: ACER Press.

Dewey, John. *How We Think.* Chicago: Regency, 1933.

Faust, Wayne E. "A Model for Effective Adult and Adolescent Education in a Relational Mode." *Religious Education.* Vol. 93, Issue 4, p. 467-487, 1989.

Favers J. and Kerssen, Jeff. "The Seven Dwarfs and Class Discussion: Archetypes help identify student participation styles." In *The Teaching Professor.* Vol.16, No. 4, 2002.

Felder, M. R.. *Matters of Style.* (1996), (ASEE Prism, 6(4), 18-23 Dec. 96) http://www.ncsu.edu./felder-public/papers/LS-pRISM html

Fuhrman B. and Grasha, A. *A Practical Handbook for College Teachers.* Boston: Little, Brown and Co., 1983.

Griffin, Virginia R. "Holistic Learning/Teaching In Adult Education: Would you play a one-string guitar?" In *The Craft of Teaching Adults: Culture Concepts,* edited by T. Barer-Stein and J. A. Draper. Toronto: 1993.

Hill, J. *The Educational Sciences.* Brookfield Hills: Oakland Community College Press, 1976.

Kiersey David. *Different Drummers.* http://Keirsey.com/Drummers html, 1998.

Kolb, D. A. *Experiential Learning: Experience as the source of Learning and Development.* Englewood Cliffs: Prentice Hall, 1984.

Kolb, D. A. *The Learning Style Inventory: Technical Manual and Self-scoring Test and Interpretation Booklet.* Boston: McBer and Co., 1976.

Kramp, M. K. and Humphreys, W. L. "Narrative, Self-assessment and the Reflective Learner." In *College Teaching.* Vol. 32, No. 3.

Knowles, M. S. *The Adult Learner: A Neglected Species.* 4th Ed. Houston: Gulf, 1990.

Lannery, James F. "Teacher As Co-conspirator: Knowledge As Authority in Collaborative Learning." In *Collaborative Learning: Understanding Processes and Effective Technique. New directions for Teaching and Learning #59,* edited by K. Bosworth and S. Hamilton. San Francisco: Jossey-Bass, 1993.

Lee, G. and Barnett, B.G. "Using Reflective Questioning to Promote Collaborative Dialogue." *Journal of Staff Development*. Vol. 15, No. 1, 1994.

May, C. and May, G. *Effective Writing: A Handbook for Accountants*. 4th Ed. New Jersey: Prentice Hall International, 1996.

McClanahan, E. B. and McClanahan, L. L. "Active Learning in a Non-majors Biology Class." In *College Teaching*. pp. 92-96, 2002.

Mezirow, H. and Associates. *Fostering Critical Reflection in Adulthood: A guide to Transformative Learning*. San Francisco: Jossey-Bass Publishers, 1990.

Svinichi, M. D. and Dixon, N. Y. "The Kolb Model Modified for Classroom Activities." In *College Teaching*. Vol. 35, No. 4, 1985.

APPENDIX 1

A New Beginning

INTRODUCTION

A NEW BEGINNING

The movie *Angel Eyes* (2001, with Jennifer Lopez, Disney Enterprises Inc.) is about a man, Catch (Terrence Carvezel), who lost his wife and son in a car accident. He survived, yet suffered from amnesia. Catch met a woman police officer and they began a unique relationship as he posed as her guardian angel. He knew he had seen her somewhere before, but could not remember where, or under what circumstances. After dating for awhile, without revealing who he was, they went to a music show. At this show, he picked up a trumpet and began to play it very well. One of the musicians recognized him and called him by his real name, Dan. He denied he was that person. The police officer he was dating took his name, searched computer records, and discovered his past. She remembered she was one of the officers at the scene of his accident. After this, she took him to the cemetery where his wife and son were laid to rest. It was there that Catch began to remember his past and the fatal accident. He was bitter and wanted to shut out this memory. Later he went back to the gravesite. He spoke to it as if to his loved ones. As he wept, he asked them for forgiveness for his neglect of them and for the accident. He faced his past as he asked for forgiveness. Later, he began to function normally again and honestly started a new life. He was able to take up his instrument and play again. He dealt with the past and then put it behind him. He was now able to live life to the fullest.

This story is a picture that is similar to experiencing new life in a personal relationship with Jesus Christ. Although we cannot forget our pain, we can face it and ask for forgiveness, and then move on to live life to the fullest.

DISCUSSION QUESTION

Have you ever felt you needed to get a new start in life?

PRESENTATION

Life in Christ begins when we enter into a personal relationship with Jesus Christ. This is the starting point of developing a life that is fully committed to Him. Life in Christ begins by dealing with your past and taking on a new way of living. We will explore what the Bible says about beginning a spiritual life, and we will discover how everyone can experience a life lived to the fullest.

"God saved you by his special favour when you believed. And you can't take credit for this; it is a gift from God. Salvation is not a reward for the good things we have done, so none of us can boast about it." Ephesians 2:8-9 (NLT)

DISCUSSION QUESTIONS

-What does it mean to be "saved"?
-What is this special favour?
-What is the danger of not accepting salvation?

-What do we have to believe?

We need to understand that salvation is a gift. We cannot buy it. We are saved by "grace." We must believe that Jesus died for our sins and that He rose from the grave. He is now in heaven.

In beginning a personal relationship with Jesus Christ, it helps to study the story of Nicodemus, a man who had a change in lifestyle, a change in thinking, and a change for the future when he believed that Jesus was his Saviour. We must now try to apply this lesson to our lives.

APPLICATION

Nicodemus was a man who had an experience that resulted in a new beginning. He came to Jesus out of curiosity. He was searching for information and change. Nicodemus was a Pharisee, a ruler of the Jews. He was a very learned, religious man. He came to Jesus by night, acknowledging that Jesus was sent from God. Nicodemus' question of Jesus was one that many people have asked through the centuries. "What does it mean to be born again?" Nicodemus was seeking to understand Jesus, His miracles, and His purpose, and how these fit with Nicodemus's already very religious lifestyle.

-Read John 3:1-21
-Why do you think Nicodemus was seeking information? What did he need to know?
-Why did he address Jesus as "Rabbi" (in the King James Version?) What does Rabbi mean?
-How did Jesus explain the way to a new life?
-What did Jesus mean by being "born again?"
-What is Jesus' purpose of coming into the world?

Once we understand this story, we can relate it to times in our lives when it was necessary to make a substantial change in direction, perhaps a career or a change in lifestyle. We too can begin again.

EXERCISE

- How does "born again" in John 3 have any resemblance to Dan's story?
- What did Dan have to do to begin a new life? What did Nicodemus have to do to begin a new life?
- What does this tell you about how you can begin Life in Christ?
- Using the continuum below, place yourself where you are in discovering a personal relationship with Jesus Christ, and what has brought you to this point.

-10 -9 -8 -7 -6 -5 -4 -3 -2 -1 ✝ +1 +2 +3 +4 +5 +6 +7 +8 +9 +10

Atheist   Trust Christ   Life dedicated to Christian service

We may desire to feel the love of Christ more deeply, as we read John 3:16. It tells of God's sacrifice of giving His only son to die for our sins. All we need to do is take a step of faith and believe in Him to have eternal life. After this, we need to follow His example in obedience.

FOLLOW-UP

We are always in a state of change through life-long learning. In the story of the Ethiopian eunuch, Philip had been sent to help the eunuch understand the scriptures. In Acts chapter 2 verse 38, Peter instructed the early Christians to repent and to be baptized in the name of Jesus Christ for the forgiveness of sins.

Here are some steps you can take to begin your Life in Christ:

1. Know that Jesus Christ is the only Way to God.

"For God so loved the world that He gave His only Son, so that everyone who believes in Him will not perish but have eternal life" (John 3:16 NLT). You can begin a personal relationship with Christ right now by sincerely praying a prayer something like this:

"Lord Jesus, I want to be born again. I want a new start in my life. I acknowledge that you died on the cross for my sin. I confess my sin to you. I admit I am a sinner. I ask you to come into my life and forgive me of these sins. Please take control of my life. I give my life to you. Thank you for your Holy Spirit who has made my life new today. AMEN."

Scripture verses to remember:
1. "For there is only one God and one Mediator who can reconcile God and people. He is the Man Christ Jesus. He gave his life to purchase freedom for everyone. This is the message that God gave to the world at the proper time" (1 Timothy 2:5-6 NLT).
2. Accept the assurance of eternal life.

Jesus said, "I assure you, those who listen to my message and believe in God who sent me have eternal life. They will never be condemned for their sins, but they have already passed from death into life" (John 5:24 NLT).
3. Feel accepted by God's grace.

"God saved you by his special favour when you believed. And you can't take credit for this; it is a gift from God. Salvation is not a reward for the good things we have done, so none of us can boast about it" (Ephesians 2:8-9 NLT).
4. Feel the release that comes from knowing your sins are forgiven.

"He is so rich in kindness that he purchased our freedom through the blood of his Son, and our sins are forgiven" (Ephesians 1:7 NLT). The apostle Paul said, "For the wages of sin is death, but the free gift of God is eternal life through Jesus Christ our Lord" (Romans 6:23 NLT).
5. Know that your new life in Christ is the beginning of a personal transformation

"What this means is that those who become Christians become new persons. They are not the same anymore, for the old life is gone. A new life has begun!" (2 Corinthians 5:17 NLT)

Which of the above steps do you feel you need to experience?
Pray a prayer of thanksgiving.
Be thankful to God for a new beginning for your life!

If you have already made a commitment, but feel you need to renew it, pray a prayer for a second chance at a new start.

GROWTH AND APPLICATION

Monday

Read John 15:1-17, The Parable of the Vineyard
Abiding in Christ
To abide means to, "be obedient to", "to bear patiently", "to remain stable", and "to endure without yielding." This signifies that we should continue in prayer and worship, confess our sins to God, and be thankful always.

How can we plan to ensure that we continue to live a life in Christ on a daily basis?

Tuesday

Read John 8:1-11
A fresh start for continuing a life in Christ
People today continue to live a life in Christ. Ordinary people like you and me can tell the story of our new beginning in Christ. We can also live our lives in such a way that others may see the love of Jesus in us.

What does this passage of scripture tell us about the fresh start we can really have?

Wednesday

Read Matthew 6:5-18
Developing Spiritual Discipline
Experiencing life in Christ means that we need to do our part in staying connected to God. Disciplines such as talking to God regularly in prayer, personal and corporate worship, and confession of our sins will keep us on track. We need to go to Him with our requests. Remember, He will supply our needs.

In this busy world, how can we reserve some special time to go to Christ?

What principles about prayer can we discover from this passage?

Thursday
Read John 15:1-21
Bearing fruit
The parable of the vineyard has meaning for our lives. We are continually in a state of change and growth. Just like the vine, we can bear fruit.

What does Jesus mean by pruning in our spiritual lives? How do we bear fruit?

Friday
Read Psalm 1
Walking with God
Remember how we said "to abide" means to "be obedient to", "to bear patiently", "to remain stable", and "to endure without yielding". Once we accept Jesus as our Saviour, we are expected to follow His example and His commandments. Jesus, through His messengers, prescribed how we should try to walk in Christ and be Christ-like.

What does this passage tell us about the person who puts God first?

What are some common principles and themes in Psalm 1 and John 15:1-21?

What does Acts chapter 2, verse 38 recommend?

Printed in the United States
42200LVS00003BB/1-153